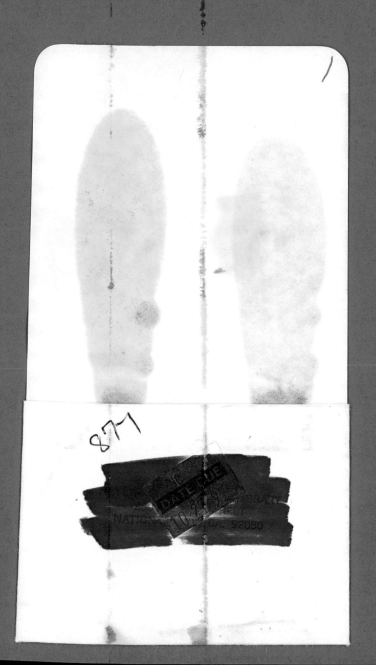

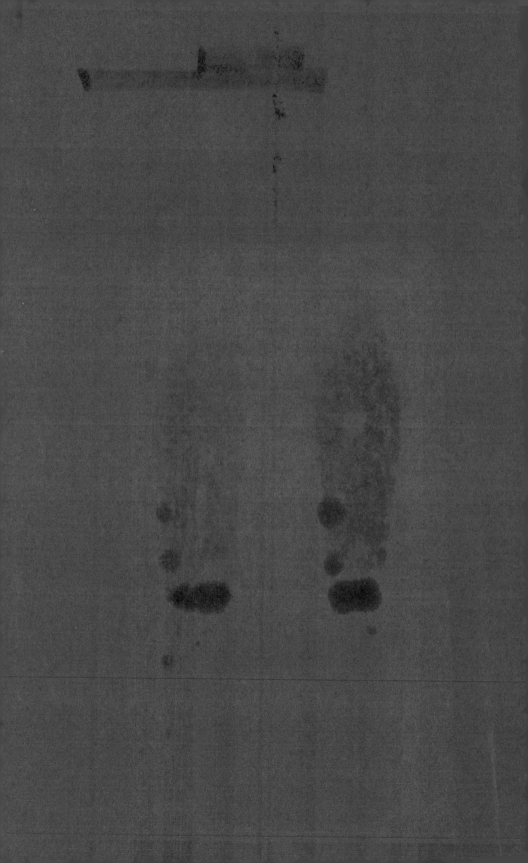

My Bike

&

Other

Friends

VOLUME II OF BOOK OF FRIENDS

HENRY MILLER

CAPRA PRESS SANTA BARBARA

1978

ACKNOWLEDGMENTS:

Cover photo with permission of *Playboy*;
Photos of Harolde Ross, Bezalel Schatz, Vincent Birge, Joe Gray, and Henry Miller on bicycle from Henry Miller's collection;
Photo of Emil White by William Webb, of Ephraim Doner by Pat Pence, of Jack Garfein and Henry Miller by Capra Press.

LIBRARY OF CONGRESS CATALOGING IN PUBLICATION DATA

Miller, Henry, 1891-
   My bike and other friends.

   Continues the author's Book of friends.
   1. Miller, Henry, 1891-   —Friends and associates. 2. Authors, American—20th century—Biography. I. Title.
PS3525.I5454Z5236   818'.5'209   77-18967
ISBN 0-88496-075-7
ISBN 0-88496-076-5 pbk.
ISBN 0-88496-081-1 lim. ed.

CAPRA PRESS
631 State Street
Santa Barbara, CA 93101

TABLE OF CONTENTS

MY BIKE & OTHER FRIENDS

Harolde Ross in 1918.

Chapter One

HAROLDE ROSS

It was the time of Freud and the swarm of neuroses he let loose upon the world. Now we know what was really in Pandora's box.

The period I refer to was from 1910 to 1924. What an exciting, glamorous epoch it was. No drugs, no hippies; at the worst only booze artists and con men.

It's the period of the glorious silent films with so many illustrious stars of all sorts. Chaplin and Greta Garbo are in the van. They are immortal, as perhaps some of the great comedians also are.

It was also the period of World War I, one of the most horrible wars ever waged. One has only to mention the name Verdun to relive it. Imagine a No Man's Land between the two sides piled high with cadavers and that an assault by either side meant first clambering over the dead bodies of one's comrades. (But in ancient times there was the battle of Platea where between dawn and midnight one hundred thousand men were slaughtered in hand-to-hand combat.)

There was just time enough to catch glimpses of Eleanor Duse, Sarah Bernhardt and Mei lan Fang, the famous Chinese actor who played women's roles better than they could play them themselves.

In the midst of all this I became acquainted with a rare bird from Blue Earth, Minnesota. Harolde Ross, pianist, music teacher, later orchestra leader also. He knew my wife before me. He always brought a portfolio of music with him; on his way home he would read the scores of Brahms, Beethoven, Scriabin as one might read a book.

He always arrived looking fresh as a daisy, his face red from being scrubbed with soap and water. A bit of corn still clinging to his ears. The picture of enthusiasm. Always something of interest up his sleeve—perhaps about Nijinsky, about Dreiser's latest novel, or the latest acquisition at the Met. Never about boxing matches or wrestling bouts or six-day bike races. To these events I went alone or with one of my "vulgar" cronies, as they were usually referred to. He never once accompanied me to the opera either, that I can recall.

During the war period, while working in my father's tailor shop, I made the acquaintance of an elderly man who took a fancy to me. His name was Alfred Pach, and he was in the photographing business with his brothers. They boasted of having been photographers to every President of the U. S. from Lincoln on down. Alfred Pach was an eccentric. He refused to handle money. Thus for all his needs he bartered. He even exchanged photographs for the tailor-made suits and fancy vests he got from my father.

One day I happened to tell him I was going to the Met that evening to hear Caruso and Amato. I told him I would stand in line to get a ticket, something I did fairly frequently and usually on an empty stomach. This led to a vivid discussion about music. When I told him I had been playing the piano for ten years or so he was enchanted. It so happened that this dear old man could get seats free for the opera or piano recitals or nearly any musical event. It was thus I saw Nijinsky in his most famous ballet, not quite realizing then what an unusual opportunity had been placed in my hands. Needless to say, I took full advantage of the old man's kindness. What celebrities I saw and heard! Among them Paderewski, Toscannini, Pablo Casals, Jan Kubelik, Alfred Cartot, John McCormack, Schumann-Heink, Mary Garden, Geraldine Farrar, Tetrazzini, and dozens of others. The one great artist I failed to see but heard on recordings was Sirota the Jewish cantor. What delicious moments I spent alone with him in our funeral parlor when I was madly and sadly in love with Una Gifford! To this day, when I hear his voice, I burst into tears. Perhaps the only vocal music I dare to put beside his is Tristan and Isolde, especially the Love Death.

For me the opera was the thing, though it was the Jazz Age, and the Roseland Dance Hall was doing a rollicking business, as was Small's up in Harlem. But to get back to Harolde Ross . . . For an opener it was always Percy Grainger's "Country Gardens." Despite all the great music I have heard it is this tune which lingers in my memory. Hearing him play it, which he did with gusto, was like saluting the flag.

During his visits to New York he always had to see his friend Ostergren who introduced me to the works of Knut Hamsun, whose name at that time was unknown to me. Being of Norwegian descent Ostergren would point out some of the grosser errors in the English translation . . . (or do I imagine all this?). I do recall with certainty that the first book of Hamsun's I read (*Hunger*) was put in my overcoat pocket by my wife as I was boarding a train to New York from Rochester.

When I look back upon this period New York seems like it was a very civilized place. It had everything—it also had electricity in the air. Harolde Ross was particularly appreciative of it, coming as he did from Blue Earth. To me, on the other hand, Blue Earth seemed a fascinating place, maybe just because of the name.

It was the time of the silent screen—Laurel and Hardy, etc., *and* the *Wurlitzer!* Political leaders are never leaders. For leaders we have to look to the Awakeners! Laotse, Buddha, Socrates, Jesus, Milarepa, Gurdjiev, Krishnamurti.

Marie Corelli put down both men *and* women! 101% Christian—a fanatic. Beneath the archaic writing was a content of great import. What matter if she were of her time or not? She was beyond "the times." She wrote from the guts, which is always in vogue.

But to get back to music. I discovered a list of all the musicians I had heard in those days. It's a formidable one and somehow fits in with my days of hunger and nights of imaginary love. I notice I had overlooked Paderewski. What an oversight! And to think that later on, during my third marriage, my Polish wife would make a little speech to him in some New Jersey town because her old man was a great Polish patriot. Then there was the beloved John McCormack, the tenor who endeared himself to all who heard him. At my parents' silver wedding anniversary I put one of his records (*MotherMachree*) on the phonograph instead of playing something on the piano.

The fact that my then wife was a pianist and gave piano lessons (I was one of her pupils) had nothing to do with my craving for music, both good and bad. One night I am at the opera, the next night at the Roseland Dance Hall, swooning over Fletcher Henderson's band. One night I would be raving about Toscanini, and the next night watching a wrestling match (usually when my favorites were on the card—Jim Londos and Earl Caddock the man of a thousand holds). This very night (1977) I will sit before the television to watch the wrestling matches praying fervently that Mil Mascaras will be on hand to show his prowess.

This period I speak of was also the day of the silent films. In addition to Greta Garbo, there were such stars as Nazinova, Olga Petrovna, Anna C. Nillson, Marie Doro, Alice Brady, Clara Kimball Young, to name but a few. On stage there were other stars, like Jeanne Eagels, Minnie Maddern Fiske,Leonore Ulric, Mrs. Leslie Carter and a host of others. Things were happening all the time. The first World War changed all this. The world has never been the same since.

At that time Harolde Ross was learning French, of which language I knew not a word. During this time I was employment manager of the messenger boys for the Western Union. One day I received in the mail a manuscript from Harolde Ross. He had translated for me a novel called *Batouala* by a René Maran. (I was then reading in translation such French authors as Anatole France, Pierre Loti, André Gide, and so on.) Did I perhaps already divine that I was soon to spend time in France?

At that time the two actresses I cared for most were Elsie Ferguson and Elsie Janus. Harolde often took my wife to the theatre or a concert. He had excellent taste and we would talk for hours on end about the authors, the plays, the musicians we adored. It was not like nowadays when one devours a book all by himself and throws it in the waste basket next day. No, men like Dostoievsky, Hamsun, Jack London, meant something to us. They were part of our daily thoughts—we lived by them. And so it was with certain actors, whether great or not. Who could ever forget Emil Jannings (especially in *The Last Laugh?*) or David Belasco, Sessue Hayakawa, Holbrook Blinn or for that matter Anna Held and Fritzi Scheff, and Pauline Frederick? Then there was the Theatre Guild, spawned from the Washington Square Players. What marvelous foreign plays which we so thirsted for.

Andreyev, Tolstoi, Gogol, Georg Kaiser. "Gas I" and "Gas II," etc., etc.

And in the midst of it all comes the Russian Revolution. LENIN. Done with Prince Kropotkin and the Anarchists. Now it's Trotsky, whom I used to see in a tea room on Second Avenue, N. Y. Now everything is really topsy turvy. The future is precarious, to say the least. Our good writers, like Theodore Dreiser, Sherwood Anderson, Eugene O'Neill seem suddenly to have dropped out of consciousness. We are reading Russian novelists—new ones created by the Communist revolution. In China, Sun Yat Sen has become the rage and my friend Bennie Bufano will visit him, come back and make a statue of him to be placed conspicuously somewhere in San Francisco. Bennie, the wonder boy from Sullivan St., New York. Never a cent in his pockets, but roaming the world.

About this time too the Six-Day Bike Races came to an end. Incidentally, I don't remember Harolde ever accompanying me to any sporting event. He wasn't as crazy as I who would go to Staten Island to watch the middle-weight fighter Stanley Ketchel train outdoors for his coming fight with Jack Johnson. It never even occurred to me to ask him to go along with me. I accepted him just as he was and he did likewise with me. (A good basis for either marriage or friendship!)

Always after he returned to Blue Earth I would receive a slew of letters from him, always on the same yellow paper. (Which reminds me of the canvases Stieglitz gave to John Marin and which lasted him all his life.)

In that period H. L. Mencken was something of a god to us. Mencken and Bernard Shaw. It was the fashion among us "intellectuals" to deride everything American. Mencken himself had coined a whole list of pejorative expressions to characterize the

American yokel. But he had also written a great book called *The American Language*. Years later, on my return from France, I received a phone call at the Royalton Hotel. It was Mencken, asking if he could see me for a few minutes. He was most humble and most affable. He had protested the banning of my books, he told me. He was very flattering and left me in a state of confusion since I was not used to receiving praise from my American literary critics.

It was the period of the Hippodrome and the trial of Evelyn Nesbitt. Yes, and of *Pelléas and Mélisande*, of Mary Garden in *Thais*, Gadski as Brunhilde, Schumann-Heink, Frank Kramer, the champion bike rider. There were also such famous ones as Ben Ami, who came from the Bowery to play in the Theatre Guild. From Russia came not only Nijinsky, but Boris Godunov and Nastasya Filipovna, from Dostoievski's *Idiot*. There was also, besides Eleanora Duse, the immortal Pablo Casals. It was also the time of the giant blimp, the Graf Zeppelin, which burst into flames at its hangar. Along with John Drew, a matinee idol, there were men such as Rudolf Valentino, Sir Thomas Lipton and the yacht races. Lillian Russell and her lover, the man with two stomachs—Diamond Jim Brady.

There were also women writers like Edna Ferber and Fanny Hurst. And still a handful of people who had read Marie Corelli. Not the least of all there was the Houston Street Burlesk. (I can still recall the features of the orchestra leader with the red hair, who played the piano intoxicatingly.) Then too there was the famous Armory Show where Marcel Duchamp exhibited his "Nude Descending the Staircase."

My father had not yet begun bar hopping with the great Jack Barrymore. But they would shortly. And it would be from Barrymore himself that later I would learn what a wonderful companion my father was, though *un inculte*, as the French would say.

When I think of it, New York at this time was filled with incredible female beauties. They came from all over the earth. There is one grand figure I must not forget—Rabindranath Tagore, a man revered and talked about as much or more than Krishnamurti. I had to go to hear him speak at Carnegie Hall, soon after his arrival in America. This time Harolde accompanied me. For he too was a devotee of Tagore. What a deception was in store for us. The lecture consisted largely of a denunciation of America, but in a piping, whining voice which rendered his words into one long, continuous petty complaint. We were miserable, the two of us, to behold our idol turn to clay before our eyes. But with the years which passed since then, my reverence and admiration for the man has increased. What he wrote and accomplished in a lifetime are incontestably of a superior order.

And how can I ever forget the day Charles Lindbergh flew the Atlantic in his monoplane—with the whole wide world gasping with astonishment? A real red letter day in American history.

And what became of my good friend during all this time? For one thing, he left Blue Earth and settled in Rochester, Minnesota, always teaching piano, always leading a small orchestra. And writing me on the same yellow stationery as always. Today he is in a nursing home there, but he has a piano in his room. He never says what ails him—I imagine it is just old age, as with yours truly.

Here was, or still is, a self-educated man cultured to the fingertips, yet living in the sticks all his life. What we shared together is unforgettable. He enriched my life indelibly. I wonder sometimes if he still plays Percy Grainger's "Country Gardens."

Big Sur, ca. 1950. Top to bottom: Henry Miller, Bezalel Schatz, Henry's daughter, Valentine.

Chapter Two

BEZALEL SCHATZ

I never heard any one call him Bezalel; it was always Lilik. Somehow just as Picasso's name suited him, so did Lilik suit Lilik. I use the past tense in referring to him because it is long since I have seen him—somewhere in Southern France at a railroad junction was the last time—perhaps twenty or more years ago. Actually Lilik lives in Jerusalem. He was born there, and went to school there. But it was in Big Sur where I first met him. He came to me on my birthday, beaming all over, and full of a project which he was determined to interest me in. It became the *Night Life* book which we did together. A beautiful and most unusual piece of collaboration, if I may say so myself. As with Lawrence Durrell, I was immediately taken by Lilik. He radiated health, vitality, optimism. He was irresistible. It took him no time to persuade me to do this book with him. (I still have a few copies left of this limited silk screen edition.) It was Lilik who did the major work. Not only did he do the illustrations and the lay-out, but he did all the silk screen pages himself. I think it took him almost two years to complete the job. Had it required ten years it would have made little difference to Lilik. His extraordinary good health enabled him to work twice as hard as the ordinary man. Besides, he also had that rare gift—faith. He never undertook anything which he did not wholly believe in. Once launched upon a project, he was like an avalanche. Nothing could deter or swerve him.

At this point I should like to say a few words about his education and up-bringing. To begin with, he was fortunate to have as parents a father who had been the court sculptor to the King of Bulgaria and a mother who was a writer and intellectual who had fled Czarist Russia. Two liberal, creative and indulgent parents. It was his parents, in fact, who brought the first piano to Israel. His schooling was of the best, in my opinion. Dancing, acting, music, athletic games took precedence over history, grammar and the sciences. He emerged from school a well coordinated individual, at peace with himself and the world (he had close friends among the Arabs and spoke Arabic after a fashion). He was an excellent soccer player as well as tennis player and between times learned to play the violin. What a difference, such a bringing up, from that of *our* children! In his teens he was reading the world's classics—Dostoievsky, André Gide, Thomas Mann, Anatole France and such like. *All in Hebrew*. It was at his home that there came people like Einstein and Eleazar ben Jehuda, who made Hebrew a living language, the father of Zionism; the painters Marc Chagall, Diego Rivera, and so on. He never became a chauvinist, though he loved his country and was at home in it. Of course, it was at this wonderful school where he learned to draw and to paint. Today his work may be seen everywhere.

Somewhere along the line he lived and worked in Paris. Which made the tie between us even stronger. In addition to French he spoke German, Russian and Polish, to say nothing of English and Hebrew. (But no Yiddish!) In many, many ways, Lilik was thoroughly unlike a Jew or even an Israeli. He was truly a citizen of the world, at ease wherever he found himself.

When I first met him he was living in Berkeley. As my wife Eve's parents also lived in Berkeley I would visit him there occasionally, especially during the production of *Into the Night Life*. But a couple of years later he moved to Big Sur with his wife Louise who was the sister of Eve, who was to become my third wife. Thus we became brothers-in-law as well as good friends. In Big Sur Lilik was to become my helpmate. For, in addition to his cultural and creative education, Lilik was also a fixer. If you had an odd job to do you could call on Lilik. He was always available, always willing, and often had original ideas as to how this or that should be done. I can never get over all the positive qualities and attributes he had. He was really a self-sufficient man. His only difficulties were with the British government officials. (Israel had not yet become a nation at this time.) This situation only sharpened his wits. He never allowed the situation to get him down. At the worst he muttered a few choice cuss words in Hebrew and Arabic. Arabic, as I understand it, is rich in foul language. (Listening to him talk to his mother over the phone I got to know one Hebrew word—*Ima* for mother.) It sounded good to me, better than mother. His relations with his mother were good, cheerful, wholesome, though in my humble opinion she was a bit of a trial. If Lilik were aware of her failings he never let on.

During this period at Big Sur I had a number of Jewish friends. They all got to know each other but I can't say they fell in love with one another. Each one was unique and outstanding in his own way. I was a friend with all of them. Often, in fact, I was taken for a Jew. All my life, as I have remarked again and again, I seem to be surrounded by Jewish friends to whom I have always been greatly indebted. Only a Jewish physician, for example, would say to a patient, a Goy like myself, that I need not pay him anything for his services *and* could he perhaps lend me a little cash? (No, I never met a gentile doctor who talked that way.)

It was while living in Big Sur, perhaps 25 or 30 years ago, that I first earned enough money to open a bank account. I mentioned Eve, my third wife. After our marriage in Carmel we decided to spend a honeymoon in Europe. (I had not been back to France since 1939.) To our great surprise Lilik wrote us from Jerusalem that he and his wife would join us. All during the years prior to my success in America I had been corresponding with a Flemish poet named Pierre Lesdain. Now that I was in Paris I thought I would look him up. (We had never met.) Lilik wanted to join us, as I had told him a great deal about my friend Pierre Lesdain. But there was one big obstacle to be overcome first, namely, the fucking British government. Apparently Lilik had to have the consent of the British Consul in Paris. That was no easy matter. I don't know how many times Lilik visited this character in an effort to obtain the necessary permit. *Why* he could not go, *why* the Consul would not give him the go signal was an utter mystery. In desperation Lilik decided on one more visit. This time he took with him a portfolio of his work to show the bastard. Immediately the man saw Lilik's work his whole attitude changed. *So*, Lilik was an artist, and his parents received such wonderful guests as Einstein. "Marc Chagall was a frequent visitor," Lilik threw in casually.

"What! exclaimed the Consul. Did you say Marc Chagall?"

"Certainly." said Lilik. "He was a good friend of the family."

With this the Consul threw up his hands. "Why didn't you tell me this before?" he exclaimed.

"I never thought it had any importance," said Lilik.

"Marc Chagall happens to be my favorite painter," said the

Consul. "Man, you could have had your visa weeks ago had you told me this. Here, let me arrange things for you . . . " And like that Lilik and his wife got permission to go to Brussels with us.

"So there was no real reason for him putting you off all this time," I exclaimed. "What a lousy hypocritical bastard! A typical Britisher. Didn't you feel like giving him a poke in the jaw?"

But no, Lilik was willing to forget the whole incident.

"I didn't tell you all," he suddenly resumed. "When I had the papers in my pocket I told him I was going with Henry Miller and his wife. I thought he would throw a fit!

" 'H. M.,' he mumbled. 'I never did care for his dirty books *but*,'—and he paused for a moment to reflect—'but I do think the bloke is a genius.'

"Then I took delight in telling him that you were not only a good friend but my brother-in-law.

" 'Don't tell me H. M. married an Israeli girl?' he cried.

" 'No, we married sisters—two Irish girls from—'

"He wouldn't hear another word. It was all too preposterous to him. He simply waved me away."

In Brussels the four of us put up at Pierre Lesdain's home. We wanted to go to a hotel but he wouldn't hear of it. He surrendered his bed to us and he and his wife slept on the floor, despite all our protests. Lesdain was one of those rare birds who, though poor as a church mouse, gave the impression of being well off. He insisted that we share all our meals with him and his wife. Happily both our wives were good cooks and aided Madame, his wife, in preparing the meals. We ate well, I must say, and the wines were excellent. The important thing, we soon found out, was *garlic*. At lunch and dinner we all joined in eating whole cloves of garlic. Lesdain insisted it was good for the health. The stench from our breath was fantastic. Add to this that Lilik had a habit of letting out a fusillade of musical farts, usually when enjoying a good meal. In fact he was capable of farting at will. He pretended to have taken lessons from that French vaudevillian who delighted his audiences with the variety of farts at his command. It included *musical* farts!

These meals in Lesdain's kitchen were unforgettable. Needless to say we laughed abundantly all through our meals. For Lesdain it was a vacation, our staying with them. He did not go to work for ten days. It must have been a great relief, for his job was at the other end of Belgium. He had to leave the house at five a.m. and got back home about ten p.m. It was a job he hated moreover. He wasn't obliged to work like a slave for he had a wealthy brother who was a minister in some branch of the government. But Pierre was too proud to accept his brother's help. He was a poet and he preferred to live like a poet, that is to say, in poverty. At the same time he displayed no rancor, no bitterness; he was almost a saint.

Of course, his brother, who was also a literary figure in Belgium, the owner and editor of a magazine of repute, insisted on showing the four of us something of his country. He had an expensive car with a chauffeur which enabled us to traverse most of Belgium in record time. Every noon and evening he selected a renowned restaurant. We ate like kings. The one town I shall never forget was Bruges. Walking along the banks of the canals I felt, as in Amsterdam, that it is only in a town of such ancient beauty that a writer should create his work. While there I wrote a piece for a Flemish magazine. Flemish is a language I imagine I could learn easily. It seems close to low German. The street signs were easy to decipher, of course. Maurice Lambillotte was the name of this wonderful host. I shall always remember him.

Among the little excursions or picnics we took with Lesdain

and his wife was a visit to the monastery which was once inhabited by the Honorable Ruysbroeck. It was at one end of a wonderful forest of beech trees about two hours' walk from Lesdain's home on the outskirts of Brussels. Brussels itself seemed to me an utterly uninteresting town, a sister to Geneva, Switzerland.

In the famous cathedral of Ghent we saw the famous triptych of Van Eyck—"The Mystic's Lamb." I was not only duly impressed, I was awe-struck.

The thing which was forever in my mind while in Belgium was that I was in the Lowlands, as it was once called. Also, although the official language was French, the people were Flemish and very proud of it.

Poor Lesdain! He was living in the wrong place. He should have made his home in Bruges, a town never to be forgotten, and, as I said before, made just for poets. Even I might have written poetry had I lived there.

I believe we went directly from Brussels to London and thence to Wells to visit my old *copain* Alfred Perlès.

Wells, as most everyone knows, has a cathedral whose façade is fascinating. Perhaps it would be more in order to call it surrealistic. Aside from that I can't recall anything else of interest in Wells. Oh yes, the liquor store! Every time I accompanied Alf to purchase wine we were obsequiously greeted by the owner of the store, a typical Englishman who always called Alf *Mister* Perlès and who was obviously impressed by the fact that *Mister* Perlès was a writer who *had lived in* Paris many years. Watching the two exchange greetings I saw my old friend in a new light. He was no longer the clown, the rogue, the scoundrel, but an English citizen, a man of standing in the eyes of his townsfolk. Of course as soon as we got out of the wine shop we would burst into guffaws. "The old fart!" Fred would say. "They're all like him here, Joey."

Though there wasn't much to do in a place like Wells, we managed to eat and drink well and laugh our heads off. Lilik, who had never met Perlès before, was taken by his wit and buffoonery. There was never a solemn moment.

Finally we decided to return to Paris, where soon after our arrival, Lilik decided that we must visit the painter Vlaminck. I was a bit surprised at first because I had the impression that Vlaminck's work had deteriorated since his days as a *Fauve*. However, like Lilik, I was curious to meet the *man*. By this time Vlaminck must have been well into his seventies. He was recovering from an illness. There he sat in an armchair a huge hulk of a man weighing over 225 pounds at least. He had always been a big man, even in his youth when he was a professional bike racer. Looking at his girth and his huge ass, I wondered how he ever managed to sit on a narrow Brooks saddle. I also wondered whether the weight of him didn't flatten those narrow racing tires. Huge as he was, he was nevertheless a sensitive, æsthetic creature. Before becoming a painter he had studied the violin and played in an orchestra.

In his rundown condition it is a wonder he received us at all. We found him most affable, most agreeable, and as he recovered his spirits a wonderful raconteur with a witty, biting tongue. He seemed willing to talk about most anything. Anything but Picasso, it seems. Picasso was his *bete noir*. As he put it in his raspy voice: "I have seen Picasso-négres, Picasso Cubism, Picasso this and Picasso that, but I have never seen a Picasso-Picasso!"

His home was now in Normandy where he owned a large farm and raised horses. He introduced us to his two daughters, very healthy, buxom teen-agers who could put away a tumbler of pure alcohol without blinking an eye.

One of the painters of his time about whom he spoke most affectionately was Utrillo. Apparently they had been good comrades in the early days, as was Derain.

I could not help remarking the almost life-size statues of Negroes from Africa surrounding the fireplace. As is well known, Vlaminck was one of the first painters in France to collect these statues. I had seen some smaller ones at Zadkine's home but never any this size. It was most impressive and most fitting.

Vlaminck did most of the talking that afternoon. One had the feeling not of being in the presence of a human being, but of an epoch. My one regret was that I had never seen him ride a bike. During the days when I attended the 6-day bicycle races in Madison Square Garden I had seen all types and all sizes but never anyone approaching the proportions of Vlaminck.

As we were driving away I said to Lilik: "Well, that's one man who never visited your home in Jerusalem."

"You're right," he replied, "but now that you mention the subject, let me tell you one man who did—I just thought of his name."

"Who was that?"

"Diego Rivera."

"That's strange," I said, "he was a frequent visitor at Anaïs Nin's home when they lived in the south of France."

We both felt like one does after having a very good meal. In fact, we felt stuffed. Later I read one or two of Vlaminck's books, for he was somewhat of a writer. There was a profundity in the books which did not manifest in his talk. As a matter of fact, one might say he was a bit cattish in his talk. One incongruous feature of the man was his mouth. It was a tiny mouth, looking almost like a third eye stuck in that huge head. Perhaps because of his illness his voice was not that of a man his size. To me it sounded thin and rather squeamish, but very effective when telling someone off or in mimicking, which he could do very well.

For several weeks we did nothing but visit art galleries and museums and excellent modest restaurants which we remembered from the old days. Then, with Fall approaching, we decided to make a trip to Spain. Neither of us had been there before.

We journeyed leisurely down to the south of France and at Montpellier we were taken by my friend Jacques Temple to meet the "great master of French literature," Joseph Delteil, who lived just outside the town at the famous *Tuilerie de Massane* with his American wife Caroline Dudley.

Perhaps I had met Delteil before, possibly through Lawrence Durrell. I definitely remember meeting him in Paris early in the 1930s when he was at the height of his surrealist fame. I remember distinctly the strange sort of baker's cap he was wearing when we met then. It reminded me of the character in that extraordinary Jewish play "The Dybbuk."

Needless to say Delteil and his wife treated us like royalty. We stayed several days in Montpellier going back and forth to La Tuilerie and sampling the excellent *vins d'ami* in his *cave*.

I suppose it was on one of those wine sampling occasions that we broached the subject of our proposed trip to Spain. Immediately we mentioned it, Joseph and Caroline asked if they could join us. (I believe Joseph had been there before, probably several times.) We set forth in two cars—Lilik and his wife in one and Eve and I with the Delteils in the other. Joseph was at the wheel. It wasn't long before he removed his jacket, keeping one hand on the wheel, and a little later his sweater under which he had several newspapers to protect him from the cold. I felt an immediate kinship with Joseph because I too am like a thermometer and barometer, susceptible to the slighest change of temperature or weather. Always turning the heat on and off.

Every now and then, as we drove through Le Roussillon, Joseph would get out of the car to ask directions. He knew the way perfectly but he wanted to exchange a few words in the *patois* of the region. He himself was born on the floor of a forest near the walled city of Carcassonne. I am sure he owes part of his mastery of the French language to the fact that he spoke Provençal at an early age. Certainly I have never encountered a French writer with his verve, wit, acuity and invention.

We visited all the famous Moorish towns as we journeyed to that wonderful town of Cordoba with its mosque and, believe it or not, a Christian church inside the mosque—a veritable defamation. As with Amsterdam and Bruges, here once again I felt was a place for poets. And here again was the sound of water, water running through the gardens, water running through the rooms of houses to give coolth. Cordoba and Granada were the high spots for me. But there was also a town, Segovia, just outside of Madrid through which ran an ancient aqueduct. There we made the acquaintance of a coming bullfighter who was practising the art of killing bulls on a bicycle in a stable. He said his parents were very poor and that if he became a bullfighter he could become rich quickly and take care of his aging parents. In America he would have tried to become a football or baseball player, in Mexico a boxer.

The principal event of our trip was catching diarrhea. It began with Lilik, who was never too careful how or where he ate. And then it struck the rest of us one after the other. Some of the toilets in hotels and cafés are still engraved in my memory.

People everywhere were warm and generous though usually quite poor. It was hard to believe that a bloody revolution had taken place a decade before. I should also mention the beautiful, immaculate hostelries, paramadors, run by the government which were extremely modest in price. Also one famous hotel, the Washington Irving, in Granada, one of the best hotels I have been in anywhere in the world. Again immaculate, comfortable and not expensive.

The only reminder of the revolution were signs on the walls of cafés saying "no singing allowed." This was to prevent political slander.

It's hard to say enough about the Spanish people themselves. Though a poor country, they retain that air of ancient grandeur, hospitality, generosity and charm which makes them unforgettable. And the government hostelries (paramadors) are unmatched in any country. They are immaculate, inexpensive, food and service excellent and the sites on which they stand always afford a spectacular view.

There is one city I almost forgot to mention—Toledo, home of El Greco. Grim, proud, haughty, oozing Catholicism, it is almost fearful. Through it, like a black snake, runs the river Tagus. In the streets there are frequent religious processions, grim reminders of the Inquisition. Yet in this austere ambiance is situated the charming abode of El Greco, adding a note of grace and levity to the grim city.

It seems to me we often separated from one another. Thus one evening Eve and I came upon a small town or village near the sea where we saw on the beach a stone staircase leading nowhere. It was difficult to determine whether the staircase had once been attached to a building or whether it was a prank by some unknown Surrealist.

Somewhere before the border we left the Delteils. We had decided to leave Spain by way of Andora, the one principality I had yet to visit. I must confess it was not an ingratiating place, but we were well treated and the food was good. Our first stop in France was Foix where we had our first good French meal. Nearby was Montsegur where the last of the Cathares had been walled up. Out of respect for their memory I got out of the car, kneeled by the roadside and said a brief, silent prayer for their souls.

We were now headed for a town which was a railway junction. Here we were to separate, Lilik and his wife heading for Marseilles, where they would take a boat back to Isræl, while Eve and I would return to Montpellier for a spell. We stood chatting there at the railway station for a long time. Finally, I divided what money I had left with Lilik (not much) and he found that by dividing it a certain way it would reduce to the number three which to him meant good luck. And indeed he did have good luck. Shortly after his return the Isrælis got the British off their backs, and established an independent nation, and began to thrive. How many eminent individuals have gone to Isræl, either for a vacation or to stay.

If I have not given much space to the Delteils it is because they went their own separate way most of the time. But the friendship formed with them on this trip has remained a solid one. Delteil has had luck, I might add. From being a renegade he has become perhaps the most notable French writer today. He continues nevertheless to cultivate his vineyard and to lead the simple life.

Big Sur, 1962. Left to right: Girl friends of Emil White, Vincent Birge, Emil White, "Florian," Henry Miller.

Chapter Three

VINCENT BIRGE

Vincent . . . good old Vincent. That's how I always think of him. Vincent never did anyone harm. That may not seem like a great virtue, expressed in negative fashion. Put positively, I would say he radiated goodness, generosity, sympathy, understanding.

To give an illustration of how he affected people let me tell how my mother reacted to him. She was on her dying bed when I happened to invite Vincent—or perhaps he had come of his own accord—to help in some way. Anyway, my mother is lying in bed. When Vincent entered the room and greeted her, she was as if electrified. She sat up in bed and nodding toward him she said, as if to herself, "If I had only had a son like that!"—and me standing right beside the bed, me the "renowned" author of dirty books, etc.

I met Vincent some years ago in Big Sur. I believe we had been in correspondence some time—he was then working for TWA and writing me from all over the world. And sending beautiful gifts too. Then, because they no longer needed radio operators, he lost his job. But soon he had another with a Texas oil company. Doing what, I never understood clearly.

From voyaging about the world Vincent had picked up French

(33)

and Portuguese and seemed very proficient. I believe he also knew Italian. He seemed to have a gift for languages.

Finally he presented himself at Big Sur, loaded with gifts for me and the children.

It was easy to like a chap like Vincent. Though he had been raised in dire poverty, he managed to go through college in Waco, Texas.

His home life had been not too good. And it left its mark on Vincent. One of his characteristic virtues was his desire to be of help—this quality, I believe, stemmed from his life at home, the poverty and neglect. For example, he was 16 or 17 before he could afford shoes. His family were so poor they rented rooms from a Negro family. In other words, the poor whites were poorer than the poor blacks.

It was in Brazil, where he stayed for some time, that he picked up Portuguese. When, some years later, the two of us found ourselves in Portugal, I relied on him entirely. His French was also excellent as I discovered when we toured France together.

By this time we had known each other several years. When I had the chance to go abroad for a vacation I naturally chose Vincent as my secretary, chauffeur and handyman. He was like a miracle worker.

One of the reasons we became such good friends was because Vincent read good books and discussed them with me. (He himself never tried his hand at writing, but he always wrote interesting letters.) He read, moreover, in three languages. He also possessed an excellent memory.

I had been staying in Reinbek-bei-Hamburg for some time because I had fallen in love with one of Rowohlt's assistants, Renate Gerhardt. While there one day my old friend Emil White showed up and then Vincent. Emil was on his way to his hometown, Vienna. Some months previously Vincent and I had picked up the old Fiat which I had left with my good friend Albert Maillet in Die, France. Vincent had driven it to Reinbek and was sort of waiting on my pleasure.

Meanwhile Renate and I had decided to join forces somewhere outside of Germany, preferably France. I then had enough money to purchase a house and perhaps a farm with it. I believe I have recounted this trip in detail elsewhere. (Vincent would remember, I don't; but Vincent is now in Louisiana and I don't have his address.) Anyway, the three of us took leave of Renate and her two youngsters, assuring her that we most certainly would find something in a few months. As it turned out, I must have been absent eight or nine months. When I returned to Reinbek without having accomplished my mission, I met a totally different Renate. She was glacial, uninterested in our odyssey, and obviously through with me forever.

Now that I look back on it all I can see that I was more fascinated by my travels than in finding a new home. We had gone through the best of Germany and Austria, then the south of France, the Roussillon in particular, part of Italy, the Ticino region of Switzerland and ended up eventually in Portugal. What I remember most vividly about this fantastic trip was Vincent's struggle with bugs—bedbugs, mosquitoes, flies, cockroaches, the whole gamut of insects. I recall vividly how, on finding a hotel for the night, Vincent would first pull back the covers of his bed to make sure there were no bedbugs. We usually slept in the same room and his bed would almost certainly have bugs whereas mine was free of them.

Once we were in a village in southern France, where Pablo Casals had lived. I had steered Vincent there hoping to meet Casals but he had already left for Puerto Rico. It was a beautiful, sleepy village and, for no reason at all, I suddenly suggested that we visit the church and say a prayer or two. We entered and knelt down to say our prayers, suddenly Vincent started up and ran out of the church. I got to my feet quickly and went in search of him. Beside the church there was a public toilet. I went in and called his name. Suddenly I saw a naked arm above the toilet doors next to the opening. "Here I am!" he shouted. "I'm looking for those damned bugs. The church is infested with them." He had completely undressed and was thoroughly examining each piece of clothing.

About bugs . . . the worst places I remember were Vienna and Budapest. There were all kinds of bugs. In Athens the moment you turned on the light in the washroom and toilet the cockroaches came out of their lairs. And they were huge and made a disgusting crackle when you stepped on them.

I forgot that we also went through Spain—largely in the rain. From Lisbon to the French border it never stopped raining, which did not prevent poverty-stricken children from standing by the roadside with hands outstretched for coins, their faces drawn with hunger and sorrow.

Well, I lost a beloved but I had a marvelous romp through Europe. I took the plane back home from Hamburg. Where Vincent went from Reinbek I don't recall. The next thing I knew he married a French girl by whom he now has a daughter of six or seven years.

Twice he has tried farming. Once in Southern California and the second time in upper New York State. In California a scarcity of water made it very difficult to raise anything. When water was discovered a year or so later, it did not run through his property. Tough luck! But then Vincent had known nothing but tough luck. The loss of his TWA job was quite a blow. (He must have had a fairly good time of it in Brazil where he picked up his Portuguese.)

It was some years later that the oil company sent him and his wife and child to the island of Malta. Malta was not a very exciting place, judging from his letters. I spoke of his tough luck. In Malta he met with the worst luck to date. He was driving home one night with his wife and child when suddenly the car dropped into an unseen hole. His wife suffered the worst injuries. The child fortunately was unharmed. If anything had happened to that child it would have broken Vincent's heart. From the time she was born he idolized her. He always sends photos of her with his letters.

Anyway, on returning to America he settled in a small town in upstate New York. Again he tried a bit of farming. Vincent had what you call a green hand. He could make things grow in the desert. How well I remember his days in Southern California when, with a tiny cup of water in his hand, he would go from plant to plant. As a teen-ager he had to get up at three or four in the morning to catch the milk truck which took him to college. When he got to school he would finish his night's sleep on the lawn or on the steps of the college. Few Europeans realize what frightful poverty exists in this country, not only among the blacks and the Mexicans, but among the white trash as well.

There were some strange and some amusing incidents during our trip. For example, in Venice, the city of one's dreams. It was just as I had imagined it from all the photos and etchings of it I had seen during the course of my life. But oddly enough, I was not enthralled, not nearly so enthusiastic as upon entering Verona. In a day or so I fell into a terrible depression, a suicidal one, and apparently for no good reason. After a day or two I decided to write a rather famous astrologer in Hamburg whom

Renate had introduced me to. Another few days passed, heavy as lead, and then suddenly at lunch while gazing at a big clock on the wall my mood disappeared as quickly as it had seized me and again for no apparent reason. That evening I sat down and wrote my astrologer friend in Hamburg. In a day or two came a letter from him saying that he knew the depression had disappeared, that he had *been praying for me!* I told Vincent, but he was unimpressed. It was some eight or nine years after leaving Renate in Reinbek that I received a letter from her telling me that the reason she had given me the cold shoulder was because our astrologer friend in Hamburg had advised her not to continue the relationship with me. That puzzled me greatly. Yet, upon sober reflection, I had to agree that he was right in thus counseling her. I had made a mess of three marriages already, with two more to come.

But to come back to Vincent and his skepticism—or should I say his common sense? Somewhere along the line I received an invitation to visit Georges Simenon. He was living in Switzerland in a rather beautiful old chateau. Emil White was still with us. I knew Simenon would not appreciate barging in on him with two cronies whom he knew nothing about. So I asked Emil and Vincent to wait for me in Lausanne. During my five or six days chez Simenon a friend of his told me of an astrologer in a village nearby who wanted very much to meet me.

I called Vincent to drive me there. The woman turned out to be another wellknown astrologer named Mme. Jacqueline Langmann. We were only in her presence a few minutes when she asked if we would forgive her, that she would like to retire to her room and work on my horoscope. I naturally consented. In the few minutes we had been there she got from me all the data necessary to make a chart. I should add that from the moment we met we took to one another like old friends. She fairly sparkled as she spoke to me. Well, in about ten minutes she came out of her room beaming, with a pad of notes in her hand. She had unearthed enough about me to give me an astounding playback of my life. (I remember now one of the things she said which impressed me and that was I should never have married. Love affairs O.K., but no marriage.) She read me like a book and, as a matter of fact, she later wrote a book (in French) about my life and chart. I was so impressed with all she told me that I urged Vincent to let her do his chart. But Vincent refused. He said it was all nonsense, adding that the planets she spoke of had long since ceased to be in the positions she took for granted. Fortunately, Madame Langmann did not waste much time refuting his arguments. Needless to say, since that day we have remained the very best of friends. About a year ago she visited me here in California in the company of mutual friends. Her book, unfortunately, has not yet been done in English. I say "unfortunately," for if it did exist in English, it would prevent many of my fans from asking the questions they do.

As I said before, we continued our supposed search for the right place into Portugal. By this time I realized that I was dreaming, that it would be next to impossible to make a ménage with two American kids and two German ones and a German stepmother.

So I returned to Reinbek and seeing that all was over between Renate and myself, I returned to California alone, a sadder and somewhat wiser man. At least I trust so. Something in my make-up tells me I will never become worldly wise. I shall always be the innocent fool no matter what crimes I may commit.

Vincent and I are still the best of friends. He goes from one job to another, one place to another, but always puts a good face on it. He is that rare thing in our society—an honest man, the man Diogenes was looking for. He is sage, broad-minded, but eschews anything that smacks of mysticism. He is a man for whom facts count, not theories, nor dreams, nor runaway ideas.

To my mind, though I hate to say this, it is just because he suppresses the dreamer in himself that life is so serious and his luck so poor. He is no man's fool, but it were better he were, in my humble opinion. One thing he definitely is, and it makes up for all his deficiencies—he is a true and loyal friend, a friend for life. And how much more important it is to be that than to be a successful this or that! God bless you, dear Vincent, you are the salt of the earth.

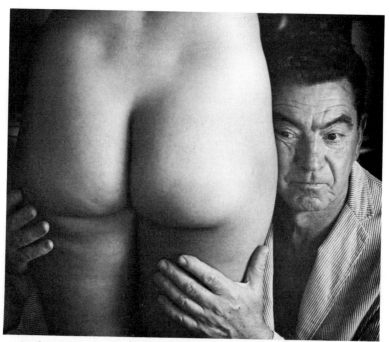

Emil and Friend, Big Sur, 1962 by William Webb.

Chapter Four

EMIL WHITE

You look into his eyes and you sense a profound, an inexplicable sadness. Yet he is a jokester of the first water and a raconteur who keeps you laughing and crying.

Which side of him is it that attracts women to him so easily? I have never decided this question, despite a long and intimate friendship. One can only shake his head and secretly envy him. For, even in remote Big Sur, his house is like a halfway station for transitory females, Orientals especially.

Of course he is an excellent cook, extremely considerate, always helpful, and truly compassionate. But these are not usually the qualities which draw women to men. Or, if they admire these qualities they do not lead them to the bed *toute de suite*. And Emil has this faculty (of quick work) *par excellence*. He has only to give a woman the eye and he knows instantly just how far he may go with her. Usually, it is all the way!

With Emil it is a curious mélange of audacity and respect. You may arrive with your wife, your sweetheart or the woman you are hoping to lay. No matter. In the space of a few minutes Emil has taken her to one side or invited her to look at his petunias or whatever, and right under your very nose he is kissing and hugging her. Absolutely unabashed and seemingly behaving in

(43)

all innocence. We got into the habit of referring to it as his "European way." This because in comparing the American and the European female Emil always implied that the American woman asked to be raped rather than wooed. Or else she was a pushover. But in Vienna or Budapest, according to Emil, to lay a woman was as natural a procedure as moving from the dinner table to the salon. It went with good food and drink, *and* good conversation. In other words the sex had to be spiced, not served raw. But why Oriental women fell for such behavior was something of a mystery.

To be sure, for all his skill and technique Emil was also a born admirer of women. He knew what pleased them, he knew where to touch them, he could make them laugh or cry without great effort. In addition his house was always something of a museum, whether it was a shack or a nice little cottage such as he now inhabits. It gave him pleasure to show a guest around. There were his paintings, his books, his photos and always somewhere a bit of erotica. Naturally, while extolling the beauty or the wonder of an object he let his hand roam freely over the fair one's body. He was especially fond of teats *and* a cute ass. He could pat one's ass so lovingly that even if she were a duchess she could not be offended. This was all part of his "respectful," even worshipful attitude. Later he would move for the kill. Often, instead of an afternoon's visit, the gal would remain a week or a month—and return for more.

We, his friends and neighbors, had all observed his tactics time and time again. Sometimes, indeed, he would seem to show off. It was as if he said to you, "You think she's hard to make? Watch this!" and he would begin operating. His manœuvres were so effective and performed so casually and boldly that we began to believe that women in general liked nothing better than to be goosed in public. Of course not all women liked this treatment. I had a few women complain that he was callous, a male chauvinist pig, and so on.

But to do him credit, most all the women who knew him loved him. And this reminds me of my first meeting with Emil. I was in Chicago, visiting Ben Abramson at his Argus Book Shop. I had never heard of Emil White. As I'm walking along Michigan Boulevard a man suddenly darts across the street to greet me. It was the familiar "Aren't you Henry Miller?" which I've heard hundreds of times. But this time it was different. Emil knew me inside out, from reading my books. (To this day he has a better memory of what I have written than I myself. When I am unsure in which of my books to look for a certain passage I write to Emil and I always get the right answer.) The sequel to our chance meeting was an invitation to have lunch with him and a few of his friends at his flat. I accepted readily, having realized quickly that this was no ordinary fan, but more of a blood brother. And so I went. To my surprise there were several young attractive women already seated at the table. They were for me, as Emil put it. Very much as if he were offering me a bouquet of red and white roses. The meal, by the way, was delightful. It consisted of cold cuts of meat, caviar and a variety of smoked fish. A treat. I took it for granted that the girls were all bedmates of Emil's in addition to being Henry Miller fans. They were all at my disposal, according to Emil, a fact which I did not take advantage of immediately. I forgot to explain that at Ben Abramson's shop I had met another ardent fan and collector of my work. He had insisted that I come and stay at his home while in Chicago. It was an invitation I could scarcely resist, being broke as usual. This individual was a University of Michigan graduate, extremely well read, married and obviously well off. He had a *penchant* for dirty books, dirty photos and pornographic films. He kept these possessions in a safe hidden behind a rolling door. Every night after dinner he would get out his treasures and display them to me. I very soon grew tired of looking at the dirty photos, but not the films. Night after night, he, his wife and I sat in the living room, with a drink in hand and watched still another film. After which his wife would tuck me in bed.

But to come back to Emil's harem. One of his girl friends who had not attended the lunch, heard of my presence in Chicago and invited me to her flat of an afternoon. She made no bones about the fact that she wanted to be laid. Having read the *Tropics* I suspect she thought I would make a good instructor. She was a strange gal, a virgin at thirty-two, and extremely passionate. Passionate *and* hygienic. If I toyed with her cunt she had a box of kleenex handy so that I could wipe my fingers. I told her I preferred not to wipe my fingers, that I enjoyed inhaling the perfume of her cunt. For some reason this shocked her. I mentioned that she was extremely hygienic. Naturally she had to douche first; then she brought a basin of warm water and washed my prick, not realizing of course that this was the usual procedure in brothels. In addition to these attributes she was athletic—almost a contortionist. She must have read up on Tantric Yoga and all the fantastic positions employed by members of the cult. For a virgin of thirty-two I must say she was a real adept. I almost broke my back trying to please her. When we had finished—get this!—she knelt at my feet and kissed my feet, then my balls and prick, and finally my belly button, all the while gurgling profuse thanks for breaking her in.

It was probably a year after my meeting with Emil in Chicago that I landed in Big Sur. I was now living on Partington Ridge in a cabin lent me by the then Mayor of Carmel. I was alone, a city lad who had never held an axe or a saw in his hand before. Somehow Emil, who was in Alaska working at some lucrative job, heard that I was in Big Sur and wrote me that he would love to join me. He offered to be my cook, dishwasher, secretary and bodyguard all in one *and* for free. I agreed and in a week he arrived, bringing gifts as usual. One of the packages contained some special delicacy from Alaska which I served to my cats, being all out of cat food. (Cats were very important on the Ridge as it was infested with rats, field mice, gophers, rattlesnakes and other pests, not least of which was poison oak.) When I told Emil what I had done he was not only shocked but deeply hurt, for which I could scarcely blame him. However, he soon forgave me and, true to his word, began helping me in every possible way.

During the lonely evenings I would often get out my water-color set and begin painting. Emil used to watch me work very attentively. After a time he got the notion that he too could paint, if he tried. He began by cooperating with me on a joint endeavor. If I made a tree, for example, he would embellish it with more bark and more leaves and branches, somewhat like Douanier Rousseau. Sometimes he would add a figure, a nude. The result was usually a monstrosity, but it gave Emil courage together with a little conceit. In a very short while he had developed a style purely his own, something bordering on neo-primitivism. People liked his work: he sold his paintings at good prices. A little later he tried to buy back some of his work. Somehow he has acquired strong doubts that he will ever paint again. Had he continued, I believe he would be famous and in demand today.

During his stay with me on Partington Ridge in that little cabin I had no car. Neither did he. One day he fixed me a sort of go-cart, such as kids make for themselves in the ghetto, and with this I was able to haul up the two-mile hill the laundry, the groceries, the kerosene, etc. which the mailman delivered to the mailbox on the road. I did this clad in nothing but a jock strop and a fedora hat.

Emil was never at a loss for words. In addition to being a good storyteller he loved to discuss politics—*world politics.*

Myself, I found politics boring. I knew next to nothing about it, but would sometimes attempt to cross swords with him, always to my utter defeat. The curious thing about this kind, gentle soul was that he was hypercritical, authoritarian and stubborn as a mule. If I wrote him a letter he would inevitably reply by pointing out what I had omitted, what I said incorrectly, and so on. He was scrupulous to a fault, exacting as a schoolmaster.

If one took a glance at his desk one would think him completely disorganized. Papers, documents, letters were piled in heaps, even on the floor and bed. But, like Blaise Cendrars, he knew exactly where everything was and could find it in a jiffy. (Cendrars once showed me a little room in his hotel which was strewn with books. They lay *pêle mêle* in a huge heap. In that disorderly pile he always stashed away a wad of paper money which he could lay his hands on at a moment's notice. This money was a safeguard against penury. Every time he made a long trip he took this precaution.)

Another thing, regarding work—Emil did everything single-handed. He had no use for a secretary. He also had a great memory and therefore needed no file cases. In short he was "the compleat Angler." He was also handy with his hands, could repair anything. The two shacks he occupied after we left the cabin on Partington Ridge were largely his own handiwork. Attached to a shack he had on the highway near Anderson Creek was a sort of open shed which served as his art gallery. It's a wonder no one ever stole any of his paintings because I don't believe he took them into the house overnight.

As I hinted before, Emil had a flair for what might be called neo-primitivism. His mania for detail and exactitude which I alluded to earlier displayed itself in his art. He could do streets and houses like an architect—a dreamy architect, to be sure. His color was good, despite the fact that he was color-blind. (It's amazing, when one stops to think of it, how little color-blindness matters in painting. Didn't Picasso used to say—"When I run out of red I use blue?") In some of his work—I think of one called "The Tiger" particularly—he evoked memories of Rousseau. Though Emil knew Rousseau's work I doubt that he was influenced by him. Like Rousseau, he tried to paint things as they are. We all see the world through different eyes and Emil's eyes were very definitely his own. In some paintings he was a poet, albeit rather a Dadaist. (See the one called "I am a Stranger here Myself.") It's in a class by itself and very Emil Whitish. Or if not Emil Whitish then Kurt Schwitterish. Why, after a few years, he stopped painting I don't know. As best I understood it, he had a perpetual fear that he could never do another like the ones before. He even bought up some of his own work. (Like a hen afraid of losing her brood.) But then some very great painters have done the same, though for different reasons.

I mentioned his obsession about *Welt Politik*. I must add in all fairness that it was not all talk with Emil. He was born in a hamlet in the Carpathians, but was raised in Vienna. During an aborted revolution he journeyed to Budapest to aid the revolutionaries. He was only fifteen or sixteen years old. To make it short, he was caught and sentenced to be shot. Lined up against

"I Am A Stranger Here Myself"

the wall, he was prepared to die. Suddenly, the guard caught sight of some Austrian currency in Emil's shirt pocket and let Emil give him the slip. Two years later he managed to get to New York where he found a relative who aided him for a while. I wish I could remember this story about the relative. It is one of his comi-tragic ones, right out of Emil's book of "Droll Stories." A companion tale to "My Life as an Echo."

It was a cruel blow which Fate dealt him twice. As one might gather from the foregoing, Emil was not the marrying type. In his horoscope there can be no doubt that as far as marriage goes he was accursed. The first wife was one of the most ravishingly beautiful women that ever passed through Big Sur. She was Hungarian by birth and had a bit of paprika in her temperament. But that wasn't the root of their trouble. It was something much worse and more difficult to cope with. It was partially the fact that she had two children from a former marriage and one of them was gaga in a peculiarly annoying way. In addition to the two children she brought along a piano which was most welcome. She had a beautiful voice and played quite well. But that one son! He was just too much for Emil. In a few weeks they had separated.

With all the women who threw themselves at him it is a wonder he wasn't married ten or twenty times. A few years after his divorce he married his second wife. I must confess that she bore little resemblance to the first wife. Whatever induced him to marry her is beyond me. To my mind she was neither beautiful, attractive nor gifted in any way. She was rather a moody, lazy creature. I said she was not gifted. She bore Emil two sons, but was no mother. Emil became the mother. Emil loved children and particularly his own. It was depressing to visit him now. All the sparkle had left his twinkling eyes. He and she rarely spoke to one another. They were deliberately giving each other the silent treatment. If you stayed for lunch or dinner it was Emil who fixed the meal. If the children needed attention it was Emil who had to look after them. He was inordinately attached to them. They grew to be bright obedient boys and Emil was very proud of them. Then one day his wife up and announces that she is going off with another, younger man to live in Australia. And she is taking the boys with her. For Emil this news was tantamount to the earth opening up beneath his feet. He was heart-broken over the prospect of losing his children and did his best to retain them but to no avail.

After a few years he decided to take a trip around the world and stop off in Australia to see his children who had now become teenagers. One may wonder how Emil, who knew how to live on ten dollars a week when I first knew him, could pick up and become a globe-trotter. (The answer to this will appear shortly.) Anyway, when he arrives at their home in Australia there is not even a bed for him in the house. He is obliged to sleep in a shed on a rude iron cot amidst a welter of junk. The children remembered him, but are not as jubilant as he expected them to be. In short it was a sad, disappointing reunion. However, from Australia Emil decided to visit Japan. This constituted a lucky break. Japan, or the Japanese, was Emil's meat. Here he met with nothing but courtesy, kindness and beauty. He fell in love with the country in no time. (I always wondered why he ever returned to America. I certainly wouldn't have.) Naturally he fell head over heels in love with the Japanese girls. One in particular he wanted to bring back to America, but her parents wouldn't let her go. I remember the lengthy correspondence he carried on with her upon his return to the States. Now and then he would show me one of her letters. Despite the halting English her letters were full of charm and tenderness. There were also, of course, quaint turns in the English—not *Japlish*, but thoughts thoroughly Japanese. One which I liked very much and transcribed on the wall of my studio was: "Thank you for always calling me darling." Certainly there is nothing wrong with the English in this sentence. But whoever heard of an American girl being grateful for being called darling? I believe he went to Japan a second time in order to convince her to marry him and return with him to Big Sur. Of course he was unsuccessful. Japan is hardly the land of romance. If anything, it is the land of love-and-suicide.

Fortunately, as I said at the beginning of this chapter, Japan came to Emil. One seemed to recommend him to another. It is almost impossible to visit him without finding a Japanese girl also visiting him, either for an afternoon or evening or for a week or a month.

In the early days of my stay in Big Sur I had many female visitors, all fans. Once I happened to remark to Emil that there were too many coming, that they interfered with my work. His ready response was: "Send them on down to my place!" Which I did to the satisfaction of all concerned. Indeed some of the more romantic fans would write me, after a sojourn at Anderson Creek, thanking me for introducing them to such a charming host as Emil White.

But I have forgotten to explain Emil's rise from rags to riches. As far back as I can remember Emil made a living selling books through the mail. The remuneration was certainly not magnificent. He earned about ten dollars a week on which he managed to live quite decently. Of course he had no vices; he never drank to excess, he smoked only three or four cigarettes a day, he needed no radio or T.V. His only vice was women, but they cost him nothing. Usually they brought him practical gifts. I think his rent never came to more than seven or eight dollars a month. He lived fairly near the Hot Springs which were then free. Here he not only enjoyed a hot bath and a sun bath but he did his laundering there too. In other words, strange as it may seem today, in 1975 Emil was living the life of Reilly. Better—he was living like a pasha.

As I said before, Emil was indeed well read. During his Chicago days he had been a frequent visitor of the Dill Pickle Club, made famous by such writers as Ben Hecht, Maxwell Bodenheim, Theodore Dreiser, Sherwood Anderson, William Faulkner and other celebrities.

I mention the Dill Pickle Club because Emil always had to do with writers. As I said earlier, he was a great reader, a perceptive one who also had a very retentive memory. I never saw him reading a trashy book, which is more than I can say for most of my intellectual friends. In addition, he was a confirmed letter writer. Sometimes, it seemed to me, he was in touch with the whole world.

In the bottom of his heart I believe Emil considered himself a writer—much more so than a painter. Perhaps his long association with writers had something to do with this. At the same time, Emil was what is called a very practical man. Not only was he a do-it-yourself man, but he had ideas of all sorts floating in his skull. How it came about I no longer remember, but one day the idea hit him to get out a magazine about Big Sur. He not only put the magazine together but he wrote articles for it himself. More, he even delivered copies of the magazine up and down the coast which was no mean job. And if people wrote in asking about the magazine he answered them himself. In this day and age what he undertook was little short of miraculous. The question remained—had he done the community a service or a disservice, for soon after the appearance of his publications tourists began pouring into the almost unknown Big Sur. I suspect that I started this business myself, all unwittingly to be sure. My letters were traveling all over the globe. Besides the fans who made my life difficult there were the occasional freaks who sometimes created untold mischief. Anyway, Emil capitalized on the fame and beauty of this Paradise and began reaping a small fortune. After a time he brought out two more "Guides," one on Carmel and vicinity and the other on the Hearst Castle. The one on the Hearst Castle sold over 300,000 copies. It was on these earnings that he was able to take a trip around the world when he felt like it. Let me quickly add that wealth did not spoil him. He remained the same modest, frugal Emil who ate the same sort of meals every day. Perhaps the one luxury he permitted himself was to buy a good station wagon which he needed to deliver his "Guides" up and down the coast from San Francisco to San Luis Obispo.

Just a very few years back he seemed to be in a bad way. He wrote me once that he had the palsy, which everyone construed as meaning Parkinson's disease. Emil accepted the situation stoically. In no way did he change his mode of life. Happily in a year or so he regained his health and now, whatever his real age, looks fit as a fiddle. His Japanese girl friends have not deserted him, nor the others either, for that matter. The one thing which remains for him to do is to write the story of his life, but I doubt he will ever do it. If it weren't for his failing sight his friend Henry Miller would do it for him. Or perhaps some feminist like Kate Millet will do it for Women's Lib!

If I were to write his epitaph it would go something like this: Here was a man who genuinely loved women despite their faults and frailties, or maybe *because* of their very shortcomings.

Ephraim Doner at home in Carmel, 1977. Photos by Pat Pence.

Chapter Five

EPHRAIM DONER

Encore un juif! (Another Jew!) But this one from the Diaspora not the Ghetto. A Chassidic Jew, b'Jesus, for which there is no counterpart in Jewry. One has to look for his equal among the Persians or Arabs—the mantic sects, what! I have never met the likes of him before. He is absolutely unique, undiluted, integral. One would like to write about him in Polish or Old French. English is too dull, too flat, too weak, to render his nature, his soul. For, of all the friends and acquaintances I have had, he is the only one with a predominant soul.

Chassidic as he is, he is always whirling about you, snapping his fingers and muttering prayers. He makes one dizzy immediately. Dizzy, thirsty and talkative. For he is an electrifier! He makes the heart and soul dilate. He turns everything topsy-turvy. Jew that he is, he is nevertheless more of anything and everything else than a Jew. Which is to say he is 101 percent Jewish. He is a Jew twenty-four hours a day—even when working on a canvas. For, no matter how seriously he takes his work (as painter), in his heart he is always *singing*—from the Bible. The Bible and Don Quixote are his two favorite books. The latter he reads every year—in Spanish. He could also read it in French, Polish, and Yiddish, if these translations were available. Though he knows five languages thoroughly, he gives the impression of knowing ten or twenty. He always knows more than one is supposed to know about everything.

I know almost nothing about his early life. I am not even certain if Poland was his birth place. It could just as well have been Minsk or Pinsk. I suspect his father, or else his grandfather, was a rabbi. No, I don't suspect . . . I am certain of it. How else could he have come by his exalted condition?

It was in Big Sur that I first became acquainted with this phenomenal being. He lived in Carmel Highlands and each week we passed within a few yards of his home on our way to Monterey to shop for the week. On the way back we would usually stop off at his home and have dinner with him, his wife Rosa and sometimes his young daughter. The latter was often a bit of a trial. Brought up by two extremely liberal parents, she seemed to take delight in expressing her rebellion. Rebellion against what? I used to ask myself. Her most daring utterances were old hat to both her parents. However, Tasha, as she was called, never could get her father or mother's goat. Their indulgence used to amaze me. They seemed capable of understanding anything and everything.

The meals *chez* Doner were always festive ones. Excellent cooks, both he and his wife. Excellent wines, cognac, whatever. But best of all, were the conversations, in which *mon cher* Ephraim usually took the lead. He was like a man out of the early Middle Ages. He could discourse on most anything. But his favorite subject (presumably) was the Old Testament, the ancient prophets, the miracles, the very language, whether in Hebrew, Yiddish or English. What a treat to listen to him dwell on one of his favorite chapters—"The Book of Job" was definitely one. He made the Bible come alive, especially for a

Goy like myself. The figures he chose to expatiate on were all grand, whether male or female. He spoke of them as if he had a real acquaintance with them. (How different, his rhapsodies, from the dull arid sermons I had to listen to in my Presbyterian Church, as a boy!) One would not know they were the same characters that were being extolled.

The very preparation of the meal was a treat to behold. For Rosa usually assisted him, one taking care of the meat, fowl or fish, and the other the vegetables and sauces. Between times one of them would go out to the garden to gather some herbs. Parsley was the key word. Never a meal without parsley or watercress. And *garlic,* to be sure. It made no never mind if before the meal the two of them had been arguing or disputing. Come time for dinner and they automatically fell into step. During the preparations for the meal Ephraim would usually give a little discourse on the "heavenly" virtues of parsley or garlic or whatever. All of which helped to whet one's appetite. At table, which always opened with a rapid prayer (in Hebrew) Ephraim would soon begin reminiscing about some book he had just read or was in the process of reading. This led to a vivacious discussion about authors past and present—Cervantes, Hamsun, Proust, Joyce, O'Casey, and, not least of all, Isaac Bashevis Singer, whom we both adored. Doner read in three or four languages, which made his observations all the more acute. He never tired of praising Yiddish as a written language. He used to make me feel ashamed of myself for neglecting to study Yiddish, or at least read translations in English. (From all I could gather, Yiddish was preferable to Hebrew, as a written language.)

The talk did not center around literature exclusively. We touched on many subjects, including astrology.

After the meat course we always had a divine dessert coupled with Cognac, Armanac or Kirschwasser. The drink would set Ephraim's tongue wagging again—this time perhaps about the splendors of French wines and liqueurs. Whatever he chose to dwell on he spoke like a connoisseur. Sometimes I suspected him of inventing things but I never caught him in *flagrant delicti,* so to speak. The same with ping pong, our favorite pastime. I cannot say that I ever saw anyone, amateur or professional, beat him. Not that he was such a skillful player, but rather that he was indefatigable, a veritable bull. (I'm sure he was a Taurean, by the way.)

A completely different side of him came to the fore when it came time to tackle the canvas. He went through a certain ritual before attacking. Here is where he displayed his holiness. First came the donning of the blue apron—with a short prayer; then the mixing of his paints. I feel certain that before he touched brush to canvas he made another prayer to his Jehovah—and that was to be permitted to do something extra good that day. Whatever he undertook it was with heart and soul.

I have only seen him once or twice since leaving Big Sur ten or twelve years ago. At that time, though highly esteemed by a few of us, he was relatively unknown in the art world. Not that that mattered greatly to him. He had been poor all his life; he took it as part of an artist's life. As a matter of fact we were both poor at the time I speak of. But Ephraim was the more resourceful of the two. On the day my wife and I went to town Ephraim would be standing at a gas station near his home, waiting for us to pass by. "How are you fixed today?" he would ask. "If you need any dough, just say the word, I can always borrow from the gas station attendant." Many is the time he slipped a ten dollar bill in my hand. I doubt that he himself had a penny in the bank. But, if he needed anything, there was always a way to get it. He literally "trusted in the Lord." And he was always protected. Whether it was through divine mercy or utter faith in life, it's difficult for me to say.

I used the word phenomenal in referring to him earlier. His ebullience, his vivacity, his never failing enthusiasm endeared him to everyone. His energy was boundless. He was a giver. If you saw something in his home you liked very much, he would say, "Take it home with you. It's yours." In this way he was never poor as others sometimes are. For the more he gave the more he received. And he could accept just as easily as he gave. Poverty to him was a sign of holiness. Though he could argue a point till Doomsday he was truly liberal-minded. He could understand the beauty and the logic of other religions. In his practice of Judaism he was universal. As I said earlier, he was really a man of the Middle Ages, learned, rounded, jubilant, forever worshipping his Lord and Master. I have listened to much talk about holiness, but it was *chez* Ephraim Doner where I saw it actualized. His little house was a refuge for those in need, who thirsted after knowledge and truth.

He didn't live long in this Carmel abode before visitors began to stream through his place. They came from all over the world and were royally received. He was literally inexhaustible. He gave himself up to his guests entirely. He never said, "I'm sorry, I'm too busy to see you today" or "I'm sorry, we don't have enough food for an extra plate." He knew how to make a little do. (The loaves and fishes, the water that turned into wine . . .)

One day a real miracle took place. His wife Rosa had been deaf for years. Then, quite by accident, she discovered a physician who promised to restore her hearing. And he did. I shall never forget her account of how it affected her to hear the birds singing again. Being quite deaf myself, I know what a heavenly feeling it is to hear birds chirping in the trees.

As I said before, theirs was a holy place. And they were protected as holy ones usually are. In accordance with Jewish tradition they never attempted to make converts. Like St. Francis of Assisi, they treated the atheist and the Catholic as they would their own. Theirs was a true liberalism, not an intellectual one.

I remember going through a marriage ceremony with Eve, my fourth wife, in the patio of their home. It was a civil ceremony, as neither Eve nor I espoused any particular religion. But it was also a religious ceremony because it was arranged by the Doners. In any case, it was a joyous, festive occasion, celebrated with excellent food and wines.

Though, as I said before, I have only seen Ephraim once or twice since leaving Big Sur the impression he left on me never fades. From him I learned more about the art of living than from anyone else. I suppose a Jew would refer to him as "a good Jew," but to me he was so much more. To me he was a good Chinaman, a good Gentile (not a Christian)—in short, a good human being. And that is saying a lot these days. Nor do I need to give my blessing. He was blessed long ago. His very presence is a blessing never to be forgotten. There was another strong reason for my attraction to Doner. He too had lived and worked in Europe. In fact, he was born there. But at some fairly early age, he had come to Paris. He knew the city, intimately. He had starved there. It's true there were other friends of mine who had lived in Paris for awhile, but they had not been inoculated, so to speak. Some who hadn't been there knew about the life from books they had read. But with Ephraim it was like doing a waltz together. One name, whether of an author, a painter, a street, a church, would suggest another. With no one else in Big Sur could I talk ecstatically about men like de Nerval, Marcel Duchamp, Vlaminck, Matisse, Utrillo, Francis Carco, Man Ray, George Grosz, Duhamel (the Salavin series) Reverdy, Roger Vitrac, Zadkine, or the works of André Gide, Anatole France, André Breton (his Nadja) and others. We intoxicated one another with our recollections. Even street names could set us on fire. The rue Mouffetard and the Place Contrescarpe, for example. Or the rue de Seine and the rue Mazarine. Or the Grands Boulevards! The Portes, the Place Violet for example. Each of us had his store of anecdotes to tell and they fell on appreciative ears. Just to mention the name André Breton was enough to cause us to explode for an hour or so. Because around Breton there had clustered a whole group of Surrealists and former Dadaists. Who in America had ever heard of Jacques Vaché, who was to have such an influence upon Breton's life? Who ever spoke of Max Jacob and his early days with Picasso? Who had read that most engaging book, ''La Nostalgie de Paris,'' by Francis Carco? Who ever mentioned Blaise Cendrars or Jean Giono? With all these writers and painters there were associated the names of streets dear to our memory, streets we had walked on empty bellies, streets (and hotels) where famous artists had lived and died. What a difference between being a temporary resident of Paris and working there as an artist! All those little restaurants where one ate cheaply—how we adored them! How wonderful to know some kind Frenchman from whom one could borrow a few francs when in dire need! How inviting the park benches when one was footsore and defeated, ready to give up the game! Yes, over those dinners *chez* Doner we relived our blessed poverty-stricken days in Paris. (Who has not starved in Paris doesn't know Paris.) Though neither of us attended church, even the churches bore gracious memories. And last, but not least, were the *clochards* and prostitutes. Sometimes the dregs of society carried themselves like royalty. Some of the prostitutes in Montmartre were like cornerstones, unforgettable in carriage and demeanor. To the great credit of the French people, those exiles of society were permitted to walk the streets, to partake of restaurants and cafés when they could. They were a very important ingredient of Parisian life.

In a sense the attitude of the Parisian was to be surprised at nothing. It was out of such a sense no doubt that one day Mary Reynolds, then mistress of Marcel Duchamp, made me a gift of my own *Tropic of Cancer* bound in human skin. (I can't recall what happened to this book. Did someone steal it from me or did I make someone a gift of it? I would give anything to know into whose hands it has fallen.)

Speaking of Duchamp, whom I have referred to as the most civilized man I ever met, I am reminded of an encounter with him I shall never forget. As everyone knows, early in his career he had abandoned painting and taken up chess. One day on visiting him at his home he asked if I knew how to play chess. I told him I did, but that I was a poor player. He wanted someone to play with badly that day, for the next thing I heard him say was—"I'll give you my Queen, a rook and a bishop, and if that is not enough, I'll throw in a few pawns."

Hearing these words I was already defeated. We began playing and in a few moves I was checkmated.

Since I had arrived in Paris in 1930 I was in time to imbibe some of the surrealist spirit. André Breton was still alive and by now regarded as the "Pope" of the movement. I had read a few of his books and was intrigued. To tell the truth, I was more impressed by Céline than by Breton. At any rate, what I am trying to say is that it was a period full of highly interesting individuals, whether sane or insane. I knew a few of these artists, such as Max Ernst, Kokoschka, Man Ray, Duchamp. Breton himself I met just once at some crazy party. A fight had broken out. I happened to spy Breton at the fireplace with his head resting on his hand, watching the fracas detachedly. He looked exactly as everyone pictured him—a lion (or a defrocked priest). Something propelled me to go up to him and introduce myself. He was warm and friendly and not at all diffident, as I had expected him to be.

I mention these incidents because our conversations were full of them.

I notice that I have given little space to Doner's painting. As I said earlier, his approach to his work was a holy one. There was beauty and sincerity in everything he touched. Now and then he sold a painting. The fact that he sold his work at long intervals did not deter him from working. He went to his studio religiously everyday—like a priest to the mass. He looked upon everything, no matter how commonplace, reverently. Whether he did a still life or a portrait or a landscape was all one to him. He admired, nay *loved* his own work. And rightly so. They all contained some part of him—heart, liver, kidneys, no matter what. And all were imbued with soul. Without soul a painting, like an individual, was to him dead. When I think back on these days, I realize that he was one of the very few American artists who understood the blessings of poverty. Though he was one hundred percent Jewish he understood and admired a great spirit such as St. Francis of Assisi. I think he preferred him to Jesus, *as I do myself.* At the same time there was in my friend Doner a touch of Don Quixote. Whatever he did had a Quixotic touch. He made even the prophets seem Quixotic—and weren't they?

In conclusion I must add that I have never known anyone

beside him who could argue strenuously for hours without getting angry. He knew always how to give the soft answer that turneth away wrath. Always, at the finish of a dispute, he was on his feet, whirling and snapping his fingers whilst reciting or chanting a prayer.

I have not dwelt on his faults. They were insignificant compared to his virtues. *Pax Vobiscum, cher ami!*

October 1977, Beverly Hills. Henry Miller with Jack Garfein. Photo by Capra Press.

Chapter Six

JACK GARFEIN

He lived his early years in a German concentration camp. Even there he was like a darling of the gods. It was there also that he learned the art of discrimination.

What amazed me about him on our first meeting was the range of his knowledge and his mastery of English, a foreign language to him. When we meet the sparks fly. He is not only most affable, charming, exciting, but a great raconteur who holds you spell-bound.

His career as a director began quite early, in New York City, with O'Casey's first play, "The Shadow of a Gunman." The school which he later established has turned out a number of excellent actors.

One is not long in his presence before one realizes that, next to the theatre his passion is women. He loves them as a gardener loves flowers. He makes no bones about it, he is a sensualist. And as such, he is like a famous violinist.

Like Napoleon, he believes that the best defense is the attack. He attacks everything with the same gusto. He is endowed with an enormous appetite for life. He *devours* things, human beings as well.

Talking to him, one feels he had an extraordinary education.

He gives the impression of knowing any and everything—and thoroughly! He probably has prejudices, as do we all, but he does not reveal them. He seems more like a "master" from the Middle Ages than a contemporary individual.

When he talks he sets everything in motion. He says things which stun, startle and confuse you momentarily.

One of his characteristics is that he seems always to be beaming, always infatuated with whatever he is doing.

Strindberg is one of his favorite playwrights. He is particularly fond of *Miss Julie*, *The Stronger*, and *Creditors*. He knows his characters inside out. Just to mention Strindberg or Dostoievsky is to set him talking for hours. Of his students he expects the utmost. He himself always gives his utmost. Besides, he is never through explaining. No matter how well you may think you know a book, a scene, a character, Jack can explain what you failed to see or understand. He is as ruthless with his pupils as with himself. He can talk as interestingly about the Talmud or the Old Testament as about modern or ancient drama.

He is tenacious as a bulldog, a perfectionist—no letting go until a thing has been mastered.

He is also possessed of great tenderness as well as reverence. In a man whose tastes are so varied and whose intellect is so keen this tenderness of his is or is not a great surprise. One thing he is *not* and that is an intellectual snob. He is so many things, always involved, always searching for answers, usually for the truth of a situation, that he has become the "compleat" human being. He is like an organ from which one can wring the finest, noblest music.

He lives on a grand scale, whether he can afford it or not. His heart is abundant and the range of his interests is simply staggering.

If I have not seen him for a few weeks he will in that time have read all the great Russian authors, for example. Or the Scandinavian playwrights. Or perhaps he will have done some research on the Gnostics. I am always surprised to learn what he has just been up to. He is, to put it simply, a cosmological man. His world is the cosmos.

His female pupils are always falling in love with him and he with them. "All for Love" is his motto.

As a conversationalist he is one of the most stimulating men I have ever known. He is always full of surprises, sometimes erotic ones, other times erudite ones.

He is deeply religious without belonging to church or synagogue. He would have made an excellent rabbi, for example, particularly because of the way he can split hairs.

Being a perfectionist he is somewhat hard on his pupils. He has the endurance of a giant and the knowledge of an encyclopedist.

I mentioned his reading. He is a voracious reader with a retentive memory. When he reads a book he knows it by heart. He retains a memory of books read which is nothing less than phenomenal. And such a diversity of reading matter! Myself, though I am no longer a great reader, I can seldom relate the story or plot of the book I have just read. But I can talk about the book—endlessly, it seems.

Jack has two wonderful children in their late teens. The product of a stormy marriage, they show no neurotic strain. Half the year they live with their mother, the actress Carol Baker, and half the year with Jack. Living with the mother they have seen something of the world. They speak several languages fluently. They are a remarkable tribute to both parents.

Jack's life with Carol Baker reminds me somewhat of my life

with one of my wives. Stormy, tumultuous, fascinating.

He is deeply religious without going to synagogue as I said before. Again, like myself, I feel. I repeat this bit about his religiousness because at first blush he gives the impression of being non-religious. A great Jewish writer said somewhere— "the man who constantly talks about God is an ungodly man." Precisely. It's when Jack is talking about some simple thing that one feels his godliness. To me he is similar to Krishnamurti, who is against masters and gurus and all so-called holy people. Was it Ramakrishna who once told his disciples not to follow in his footsteps, confessing that his love for God was a vice?

I hope I have made my point clear. To put it more simply still I would say that Jack is in love with life. But he includes *all* life. There is no "holier than thou" in his make-up. All is holy, and out of evil often springs good. *Voilà* a man after my own heart.

I mentioned earlier that Jack gives the impression of being a well educated individual. Oddly enough it began in the concentration camp. One of the guards took a liking to him and made it his business to teach him what he may have learned at school. A strange business, this tenderness among the killer Nazis, but a true paradox. On Christmas day, for example, he was treated to a piece of cake and a glass of wine by his jailers. Apparently even monsters have a heart. As a result of these occurrences Jack has a most forgiving and understanding heart. I believe it was he who once quoted a line out of Eckerman's *Conversations with Goethe*. Said Goethe one day: "I doubt that there is a crime, however heinous, that I have not felt capable of myself." This from "the first European."

Jack has a mind like a razor's edge and a heart to match. A rare combination. If he had followed his head he might have become a celebrated rabbi; if he had followed his heart alone he could have become a saint, a *Jewish* saint, *bien entendu!* But he is, as I mentioned earlier, the whole man, the rounded man, the man of a by-gone epoch. Today we turn out great scholars, great pundits, great scientists, even great musicians, but no great men of heart. We turn out men of learning who can also be monsters, masters (in a religious sense) who turn out to be fakers. Everything we touch in this world of today has something phony about it. It's the age of plastics, nothing being what it seems to be.

And now I feel like saying something that may shock some of my readers. I think that Jack Garfein's experience as a boy in a Nazi concentration camp demonstrates that sometimes out of evil springs good. Certainly I know no other way to explain his benevolence, his sense of humanity, his understanding and compassion.

After all, is it so very strange what I have just written? Do not the Christians owe their god Jesus to the treachery of his disciple Judas?

Only the other day, from the lips of a physician who had served in the war, was I informed of the fact, according to him, that over half the guards in the concentration camps were volunteers from other countries than Germany.

But enough of this . . . one may begin to think I am making a plea in behalf of the Nazis, than which nothing could be further from the truth.

What I am stressing, I must repeat, is that good and evil are mixed in the human being. We have not yet seen the perfect man, though we have had some noble examples of a human being. Suffice to say, they were not all saints. We also know that there were so-called saints who were nearer to being monsters.

To change the subject abruptly. . . . To see Jack Garfein putting his arms around a woman and kissing her is a very special treat. If it was lust which inspired his behavior then lust has to be regarded as one of the virtues.

This is only a feeble example of why I said before that Jack is a holy man. Perhaps a holy man who, out of the greatness of his heart, permits himself to sin on occasion. (And not go through the farce of repenting afterwards.) No, his behavior reminds one more of that of a Zen master whose religion is no religion. No repentance, no guilt, no shame! How refreshing!

To Henry -
Behind every great man there is a dog.
Byron & Joe

Joe Gray and his dog Byron.

Chapter Seven

JOE GRAY

This was supposed to be Chapter the Last. But I can't risk putting it off that long since my hold on life may break any time now. And I wouldn't want the "Book of Friends" to be minus Joe Gray who meant so much to me. *Meant* did I say? I mean *means*, for in my memory he is still alive and kicking, still as vivid as ever.

Joe was loved by men, women, children and animals—or else detested. Born and raised on the East Side, Manhattan, he had all the characteristics of this breed from which so many celebrities sprang. Only Joe was not what you would call a celebrity. To be honest, and this is one of his qualities which endeared him to me, Joe had no ambition. He was quite content to be a stunt man, a stand-in, a bit actor which he had become after a brief career in the ring. In fact, he would have enjoyed doing nothing at all, getting along on a small pension. That is, so long as he could go to the beach every day, read his favorite authors and have three or four good-looking women on the string. Oh yes, and his dog Byron, from whom he was inseparable.

Though his career as a pug was brief it nevertheless marked him. It had altered his physiognomy—for the better! Born with a real Jewish nose, he had had it smashed during one of his early

(77)

bouts. He didn't remain long as a fighter because very early in his career he was knocked out. That seemed to bring him to his senses. He quickly realized that he would never be a Benny Leonard, who was then his idol.

His older brother, Mack Gray (Killer Mack, he was nicknamed) was living in Hollywood and had a cushy job managing one of the very popular stars. Mack urged his brother to join him, promising to find him work in the movies. Before joining his brother in Hollywood Joe had a new nose built for him by a plastic surgeon. From a tough mug he became a handsome guy whom women looked upon favorably. And so Joe took the train and came to sunny California, which was just to his liking.

But he did not come before having one or two heart-breaking experiences with the opposite sex. *Unrequited love.* How often we discussed this subject at the dinner table. Joe apparently was one of those who never get over a woman's betrayal. It made him bitter toward women in general, unforgiving, hard as nails. Nevertheless, he was never without a woman on his hands, usually several at a time. He maintained that he never fell in love with them; he simply could not resist the flesh. He no longer thought of them as persons, but as possessors of big boobs, marvelous thighs, big asses and so on. He always took them apart immediately. I used to drive about with him sometimes of a weekend. He wanted to show me how easy it was to pick up a cunt—*any* cunt. And to observe his tactics it was indeed easy, but also rather embarrassing. What he liked best, he used to say, were maids, maids from South America, who worked for slave wages in rich Jewish families in Beverly Hills. They were "always grateful" for a good lay and a meal. He didn't put any stock in the actresses who were sitting around waiting their turn, however beautiful, even ravishing they might be. They were too proud, in his opinion. However, he often brought these glamour girls to my home—*"for you"*—he would whisper on the side. I must say I never saw such a bevy of beautiful women in my life. But, as he was quick to point out, there was always something missing in them. His contempt for actors and actresses was undying. "All they know how to do," he would say, "is to read the lines." As a generality, this was of course quite true. Most of these folk *are* empty-headed, when you get to know them. I don't think I need to indicate those who were the exception to the rule, or vice versa.

Perhaps it was his rough masculinity, perhaps it was the cute nose the plastic surgeon had given him, but there was something about Joe which made him extremely attractive to most every woman. I was often surprised by the kind of women he would bring to meet me. I should have said earlier that shortly after I arrived in L.A. I ran into Joe at the home of a mutual friend. We became friends immediately. In a way, it was something of hero worship on Joe's part. He had only just begun to read me when we met. Prior to this he was not much of a reader, though strangely enough, his favorites were Byron, Shelley and Keats. Byron he could recite by the yard.

I mention all this only to explain that when Joe did bring a woman to the house it was to give her the privilege of meeting "the great Henry Miller, Henry Miller the genius," etc., etc. It was as if he were bringing me fresh flowers.

The women, usually gullible, were ready to see whatever Joe indicated. What often annoyed him, though he wouldn't show it till after the gal had left, was the free and easy way I accepted her presence, the way I put my arms around her and kissed her, for example. Tough and rough as he was, Joe was not used to such behavior. Or, to put it another way, he probably felt the girl should have shown a little more resistance. At bottom it was a hang-over from the Puritan days, a quality which lurks in every American male. Presumably, my years in Paris had rubbed off some of this nonsense. In another sense I was far more naïve, far more innocent than Joe. He called me a romantic, not without scorn.

It would infuriate him if I said that I didn't mind being hurt by a woman, if I loved her. If I loved, I would say, I love body and soul. This made me a masochist in his eyes. Or a blind fool, or a dozen other things. None of which, however, prevented him from coming to me for advice. For, despite the fact that he was supposedly through with women, he couldn't help but get caught now and then. Of course he never took my advice. No siree, not Joe Gray. It would end up by him giving *me* unasked-for advice. What Joe liked more than giving advice to a friend was to badger and bully him. To me his antics were amusing. I would encourage him to lay it on thicker. For example, some time after I met Joe I fell in love with Hoki Tokuda, whom I later married. Now Joe took a violent dislike to Hoki almost from the very first. Unlike me, he did not see the unusual qualities in the Japanese woman. In fact, he suspected them all of being blood suckers. She was out to get something, that was his idea. I knew of course that there was a strong element of jealousy in Joe's behavior. This Hoki was going to rob him of his best friend. She was a menace. And so on. What he could not understand was that I got a kick out of his ranting. I would incite him to continue, to say his worst. This bothered him. My passivity, or endorsement, seemed to him like a betrayal of my love for Hoki.

Finally the day came, when over dinner for three, Joe urged me to marry her. "She'll make you a good wife," he said, a remark unthinkable a week previous.

We damn near took Joe along on our honeymoon, because Joe had never been to Paris and wanted very much to see how artists behaved there. (Probably influenced by *Tropic of Cancer*.)

From the day of the marriage on, he watched Hoki like a hawk. Every other day he'd ask, "How's it going?" "Is she living up to expectations?" And so on. He was relentless. Any little fault he discovered became a dramatic incident.

Soon he was telling me that he had always warned me she was no good. It was a veritable merry-go-round. Since I never said anything one way or another he assumed (and rightly) that it was a fiasco.

However, playing ping pong wiped out a lot of the bitterness. We used to play, Joe and I, occasionally joined by two or three friends, almost every day and for several hours at a time. Joe played best to the music of Scriabin's Fifth Piano Sonata or Ravel's *Gaspard de la Nuit*. He was as violent in his likes and dislikes for composers as he was for authors. As for the authors he disliked I usually shared his opinion. But for composers, no! Joe was best in his appreciation, or lack of it, for authors. For a man who had had no great education it was amazing how keen his judgment of authors was. His great favorite was Byron, followed closely by Keats and Shelley. He even named his dog Byron. For a man who could so easily ingratiate himself with women, it was amazing to observe the affection he bestowed on Byron. Byron came first in everything. Of course this lavish affection for a dog came about through some heart-breaking setbacks with women. He had been betrayed three or four times, with the result that he was absolutely adamant as regards showing any further affection toward the other sex. All his attention now centered on Byron, his dog, and me. He couldn't avoid fucking the women occasionally, but he could never fall in love

again. He was absolutely unforgiving. Having been betrayed
two or three times he was absolutely relentless in his aversion
toward the other sex. Which did not prevent women from
throwing themselves at him. To mollify them he would give
them a lay and then forget them. Yet he could not resist flirting
with them, leading them on, but he never said "I love you!" The
word love had dropped from his vocabulary. What he frequently
did was to bring his women to me and offer them to me, like a
nice bit of juicy fruit. Fortunately, his women weren't always
satisfied to take the substitute he offered.

It wasn't only women Joe brought to the house, but gifts of all
sorts. Books especially, followed by health food products, wearing apparel (often the cast-off suit of some movie star) and
usually recordings by Scriabin, Ravel, Debussy, et alia. Or a
new set of ping pong balls, for we wore them out fast. In addition
to bringing gifts for me he also brought gifts for my children,
Tony and Val.

If he stayed for dinner, which he frequently did, he would get
a little high on wine and whiskey—or sometimes Armagnac, if I
happened to have any on hand. If I warned him to take it easy
driving home he would tell me not to worry, if he got too drunk
Byron his dog would see him home safely.

One night, after imbibing rather heavily, he drove home so
cautiously that he aroused the suspicions of the police. Just as he
pulled up to his front door out came the cops and took him to the
brig. He begged them not to do any harm to Byron, offered to
pay for his board and keep, and so they set Byron free.

That was a night Joe never forgot. Tough bimbo that he was,
he was not used to associating with the dregs he met in his cell.
He emerged from the experience a thoroughly crushed individual. Had he been a devout Catholic or even an orthodox Jew

he would certainly have done penance for a month or so. It didn't stop his drinking, it only moderated it.

There was a serious side to Joe, the eternal student, you might say. Books enthralled him, probably because he had neglected them for so long. Nothing daunted him in his reading ventures. As he explained to me one day, when he began reading my books, he paid attention to the books and authors I mentioned in passing. And so, like that, he found himself reading Blaise Cendrars, Jean Giono, Ferdinand Céline, Richard Jefferies, many authors indeed whom he had never heard of a few months before. What's more, he would discuss their work with me or anyone who happened to come along. Strange indeed to hear him talk about Marcel Proust or James Joyce in his jive language. To me it added a piquant note, far more interesting than the dry verbiage of a college professor. Often, on returning a book he had borrowed, he would slap the book down and exclaim: "That's one hell of a good book, do you know that?" To which I would reply, "Yes, Joe, that's why I told you to read it." Whereupon he would say, "Where do you dig up all these books?"

A book like "Song of the World" by Giono or one of Isaac Singer's book would put him in a trance for a week.

To be honest, I never found Joe guilty of reading a trashy book. He despised people who did read such books.

On the set at the studios he always had two or three books with him. He carried them to lend if he found a good listener, or, as he would put it, someone who wanted to be healed. For Joe regarded good literature as therapy. Though Jewish he went to Temple only on Yom Kippur—out of respect, he said. Otherwise he had no use for sermons whether delivered by a Jew or a Christian minister. They were all full of shit, according to him.

Joe never wasted time talking politics or religion. Nor did he waste much time talking about films. He felt sorry for the deluded gals who poured into Hollywood every day, hoping to become a star one day.

However, his sympathy for them did not prevent him from taking advantage of them. If he took a fancy to a tyro he would play his cards like any Hollywood bum. He would promise her the earth, let alone a good part, in order to get his end in. You might say he gave her a sympathetic fuck. If he met her six months later sitting on the bench he would say, "What's the matter with you, didn't I tell you who to pay attention to? You're wasting your time, you're fucking the wrong guys. Here you don't fuck for pleasure, but to climb a little higher up the ladder. They're all bums, I told you that months ago. Not a decent one in the lot. See that guy standing over there (pointing to a well-known male star), he'd fuck your grandmother if he thought it would help him. Watch out for the wolves!"

Funny, Joe could play the seducer and the protector at the same time. And they all loved him for it. He wasn't a bum like the others. He really had a heart—and a conscience of sorts.

Playing ping pong to the tune of Scriabin's Fifth Piano Sonata—we had at least six or seven different virtuosi recording this piece—Joe would spice his talk with his latest favorite author, the cunt he picked up the day before—her teats, her ass, her thighs—together with tid-bits about famous prize fighters and the values of certain health foods which he ate religiously every day.

He got me so riled about his fucking health foods that one day I composed a list of my favorite dishes and tacked it on the closet door of the kitchen. They were all dishes inclined to increase your cholesterol—juicy, fatty, tasty bits. At the bottom I wrote in big letters "NO HEALTH FOODS PLEASE!"

In addition to books Joe loved my watercolors. He was always begging me to give him one as a bribe for this guy or the next in the casting department. For himself he was content to take only my failures—he finally plastered the walls of his joint with these.

As with literature, so with painting. Joe soon caught on to the good ones. Modigliani was his favorite, followed by Bonnard, George Grosz, Renoir and Matisse. Picasso he considered a fraud. And nobody could ever convince Joe that he was wrong in his predilections.

About everyone and everything Joe had very definite opinions. If, on meeting someone for the first time, he took a dislike to the person he made no bones about telling him so. It didn't matter if it were a man *or* a woman. With a woman he might soften his speech somewhat, but never his attitude. With a man it was a positive treat to hear him carry on. Such abuse as he handed out—only an ex-pug could get away with it. But Joe didn't behave this way because he knew he could beat the shit out of the other guy. He just couldn't keep from speaking his mind. It made no difference to him either that the person might be a friend of mine. After the individual had left he would say to me, "And he calls himself a friend of yours! How can you tolerate such shits? They're all just ass-lickers." It made no difference if the person in question happened to be a man of some prominence—a doctor, an artist, an analyst. For analysts Joe had only a supreme contempt. Instead of shrinks Joe offered people good books. He had a whole string of such therapeutic works to recommend, ranging from Herman Hesse to Jean Giono. There were certain titles of mine, for example, which he always had on hand, and would read aloud from on occasion.

He also kept a wonderful notebook filled with quotations from his favorite passages from all the books he had read. I tried to induce several publishers to take it, but they couldn't see as I did. To me this notebook was in itself the key or the door to the best in literature. When Joe liked a book he never stopped talking about it. He recommended it to all and sundry regardless of education or culture. "Read it!" he would say, "It will do you good."

Though he had begun life as a boxer, boxing held no great interest for him. "They're all fakers," he would say. "All bums." As for wrestling, it was absolutely beyond his comprehension that a person like myself could watch it on TV week after week. I would tell him that it didn't matter to me if they were all phonies, I liked it. I got more of a kick watching these fakers than listening to an intellectual lecture or watching a T.V. performance.

It was rare indeed that Joe recommended a movie to see. Sometimes he would recommend a not-so-good one because one of his buddies was in it. Joe was good friends with a number of well-known movie actors. George Raft, for instance, was one of his great favorites. He only had praise for him, no matter what the gossips said. It was surprising indeed the sort of friends Joe had—they were from all walks of life, including the best and the worst, a point in his favor, I thought. And with them all he spoke the same language. As a stand-in or stunt man for certain well-known actors he acquired an excellent wardrobe of their cast-offs. Now and then one of those $350 cast-offs fit me perfectly. "Take it," Joe would say, "it's yours." Like that, he never had to buy clothes, nor I either. (For most of my life I have worn other people's clothes. Now in my old age I was beginning to look like a dude.)

In the early days of our acquaintance Joe liked to invite me to rather good restaurants. Often, I discovered, he had chosen the place not for the food but because of a certain waitress he had taken a shine to. For a few years we went frequently to Stefanino's on Sunset Blvd. He liked the bar and the women he could pick up there. He also had a great admiration for the woman who ran the wardrobe. She was what Joe called "a real woman," a rare compliment from his lips. She was an Italian actress who had come to Hollywood, thinking to hit the jack-pot, but got nowhere. I too admired her. I thought of her as a "lady, a lady of parts."

Most everyday Joe could be found at the beach, foot of Chautauqua Blvd. He needed the sun, he would say. Actually what he went there for was *Cunt*. How often he would point out a woman of forty or so and say to me, "Jesus, Henry, you should have seen her twenty years ago when I first knew her! What an ass, what teats! One of the best lays I ever had. Look at her now. An old bag already."

At the beach he was always surrounded by a coterie of friends, of both sexes. They were drawn to Joe like flies to fly paper. To most of them he addressed cutting remarks, like, "Why don't you do something about that belly of yours?" Or, to a woman, "Aren't you getting a bit sloppy? Look at your teats—they're like two heads of cabbage!"

All of which his cronies took in good part. Now and then he would be hit up to pay for an abortion or a divorce. It didn't bother Joe. He took everything in its stride. "It's life," he would say, and begin to talk about Gauguin or Van Gogh. "Look what they took!" he would say.

Most young, striving artists he had no respect for. They weren't "serious," in Joe's opinion. All the artists he admired were dead.

He was usually in good humor. If he felt bad he wouldn't show up. Needless to say, he was always in good shape, even if he did booze it a little too much.

With all the failed watercolors I supplied him with his walls were soon filled. Now and then he would try to wheedle a *good* watercolor out of me. Anything he wanted badly he usually succeeded in getting. And so, over the years, he managed to obtain a few of my very best paintings. To tell the truth, even the failures didn't look so bad.

When he received a visit from some broad he had been chasing he always made her examine my watercolors first. Then, little by little, he would work out his usual strategy—a glass of cheap wine, a cracked Debussy recording, a nice rug by the glowing fireplace, and before you knew it, he was undressing her. Everything with Joe was a matter of technique. If you knew what cards to play you had her without trouble. If you didn't you were a loser. And Joe had no use for losers.

Every now and then he had to leave the country, as a stand-in for Dean Martin or some other star. Joe enjoyed these trips abroad. Like any other tourist he would head for the show places—it Italy the burial grounds of Shelley and Keats, in Switzerland, the castle on Lake Geneva which inspired Byron's *Prisoner of Chillon,* in Germany the lake (Starnberg) where the mad Ludwig of Bavaria was drowned. Naturally his job had taken him to many famous places. In Switzerland for example, he tried in vain to visit one of Herman Hesse's residences—the one in the Ticino on a mountaintop. Joe was crazy about Hesse's *Siddhartha*—to him, and to me too, I must confess, it was like a New Testament. We could talk about it for hours.

To hear Joe talk about his favorite authors in his own jive language was something. In this lingo he could discourse for hours on such authors as Proust, Elie Faure, Thomas Mann, even James Joyce, though he confessed that Joyce was over his head.

In passing through his bedroom to go to the toilet I always stopped a few minutes in the bedroom to look at two objects: one was a pair of boxing gloves given him by his idol Benny Leonard; the other was a small framed photo of his mother. This photo intrigued me very much. The first time I asked Joe who it was he said, "My Mother. A wonderful woman. I loved her very much. She was very good to me." Almost every time I passed her image I asked him more about his mother. His replies always made me envious. If only I had had a mother such as Joe described, I might well be a different man today. Perhaps not as famous, but a *better* man. Not to have a mother you love and believe in is a serious handicap. I have often noticed that some of the toughest bimbos had the greatest reverence for their mothers. A famous French writer whose work I adore says somewhere in his books that a man who does not love his mother is a monster. And I hated my mother all my life!

One may ask how could a man have such respect for his mother and treat women so bad? (Well, think of Napoleon.) Actually, Joe loved women though he could never forgive their betrayal. And it had happened not once, but two or three times. I have never got over the loss of my first love. I never will, no doubt. I am fortunate that I don't take it out on other women, though I realize that is exactly what some of my female readers think I do.

No, Joe was drawn to women very naturally. He accepted them as you would flowers or exotic birds. But he wouldn't trust them. *Never.*

What crazy conversations I have listened in on when trying to take a nap at his joint. Suddenly I would be awakened by Joe's cussing and swearing at the top of his lungs. I would open my eyes and find him at the telephone with a grin from ear to ear. Meanwhile he is bawling out the young woman on the other end of the line.

"You bitch! Didn't I tell you never to phone me again? What's the trouble this time? Another abortion—or what? I can't help you out any more. I wouldn't if I could. It's no good. You'll never learn. You're a stupid bitch if ever there was one. All your brains are in your cunt and by the way, don't come knocking at my door at two or three in the morning. Lay off the booze! Keep your legs crossed! If you have to, why not masturbate once in a while. It won't hurt you. Listen, I suppose you're a Catholic, aren't you? I feel sorry for you. All that shit and still you're shit out of luck. . . . "

The girl is trying to get in a few words. Joe is saying—"I don't want to hear any more about that cock-sucker. Fuck him! He's no good for you. He's an ass-hole. Why don't you find yourself a regular guy, *like me*, for instance? But don't bother me. I ain't got no time for sick cunts like you."

The girl is trying to tell him something. I suspect that she wants him to know she loves him, just him.

"I've heard that crap before," says Joe. "You don't fool me. You can't really love anybody. Got that? So long now, I'm busy." And he hangs up.

Joe never came to see me, and he came frequently, without bringing a gift of some sort. He never came in a depressed or downcast mood. He was always boisterous, jovial, full of stories. Real life stories. He had just picked up an unusual broad—what legs! What teats! And so on. Or he had picked up a writer, sometimes an actor down and out. Or something would remind him of so-and-so, a guy whom everyone in Hollywood knew, according to Joe. Anyway, this guy was known for having an enormous prick—a horse cock. The joke of it was that sometimes he would be walking with a guy, chatting away, and suddenly he would take out this huge hunk of meat and place it in his friend's hand. Joe was full of pranks too. If he detested a guy, what he called "a creep," he would take pleasure in calling him on the phone at four in the morning and say, "Hey, what's the matter with you? It's half past eight already. I thought you were going to meet me at seven." And with that he'd hang up. Naturally the guy wouldn't be able to go back to sleep.

He made it a point to have brunch every Sunday at a famous delicatessen in Hollywood where actors usually met. Joe knew them all. And despised most of them. At these gatherings there usually came a well-known film actress who was fond of dogs. "She loves her dogs more than men," Joe would say. And then he would add in a whisper, "I know she wants me to fuck her, but I'm not interested. I talk dogs to her."

When it comes to loving dogs no one could love a dog more than Joe loved his Byron. He took Byron with him everywhere. Now and then he would recite a few lines of Byron's poetry to him. This animal was quite unique, as everyone admitted. He wasn't a dog—he was partly human. He hung on Joe's every word as if it were the Scripture. When he looked at Joe it was with such tenderness, such adoration, that it was almost beyond love. If anyone didn't happen to care for dogs Joe had no use for him.

Incidentally, Joe had a habit of sizing up a stranger instantly. And, what's more, if he didn't like the guy, he would let him know it immediately. That went for any and everybody. I've heard him berate a well-known surgeon and insult a famous virtuoso. "Just because you're good with the knife," he might say, "don't carry any weight with me. You're a weasel, a nobody—to hell with you!"

If, on the other hand, Joe liked someone, he couldn't do enough for him. Speaking of the gifts he used to bring me, often it was food. Though he was not an enormous eater, Joe had a great respect for food. It hurt him to see the way I wasted food. Yet I had starved more than Joe by far, which did not prevent me from throwing good food into the garbage can when I had had my share. (I had always hated my mother's command to finish what was on my plate. Sometimes I would get up the courage to tell her that I was not a garbage can. But with stupid, conventional Germans, such behavior was like committing a sin. And Jews often felt the same way, I noticed.) It also hurt Joe that I did not relish the health foods he brought and which I never touched.

Though he was Jewish, I noticed that he didn't have much traffic with Jews. And the learned ones bored him to tears. Often he would interrupt a conversation (say about psychoanalysis) and say, "C'mon, let's have a little ping pong." For that he could have got a good crack in the jaw from a Goy, but Jewish intellectuals never made much use of their fists.

Joe was full of surprises too. Like one day he comes in raving about Montaigne, the famous French writer. (His notebook was full of quotes from Montaigne.) Now Montaigne, though highly regarded, isn't usually the subject of table talk. Yet Joe could go on for hours about him.

One day he asked me for a piece of crayon, got on a chair, and wrote on my studio wall this: "A man who marries his mistress is like a man who shits in his hat before putting it on his head." Joe signed it—Montaigne.

Joe wrote a number of things on my studio wall. One was from Céline and went like this: "I piss on it all from a considerable height." Joe adored Céline, as we all did. One day I surprised him by telling him that the French considered Céline an anti-Semite. "What if he didn't like Jews," said Joe. "He was a great writer. Give me Céline any day to some of those Jewish punks who are handing us a lot of shit."

That was Joe—always direct, never pulling his punches.

I liked Joe because he had no ambition and also because he was a self-educated man. I'll never forget the day he discovered Zen. He had a book under his arm and a wide grin on his face. Proffering me the book, he said, "Henry, this is *it*. This makes sense. It cuts clear across this Jewish-Christian nonsense. It opens your eyes, makes you laugh, and lets you let out a good loud fart. Why didn't I hear about this sooner? It would have saved me lots of agony." On and on he went, happy as a lark. Then one evening, when we were watching TV, he heard Alan Watts for the first time. The look he gave me was one of utter amazement, "Why haven't they got guys like this in the Synagogue?" he asked. "Jesus, Henry, I never heard a man make so much sense as he did. And you say you knew him once? I envy you. Here I am hanging around with all these half-assed actors, these crack-pots and shit heels." And once again he went off into a spiel about what nobodies actors are, how all they know what to do is to read the lines, not a thought in their heads, and so on.

Nobody could forget Joe Gray once they met him. He was like a shock of electricity. In the beginning of our friendship he used to haul me with him to Hollywood parties. What dull affairs! But Joe would always say, "Wait a minute, there'll be some hot-looking dames come in before the night's over." Funny thing was, he could go up and talk to anyone, man or woman, as if he were an important guest. If he took a fancy to a broad he would promise her a job, anything she wanted. He always had printed cards in his wallet, with his name and address. As the night wore on he was handing out his cards like laundry tickets. It was amazing to me how many girls kept his card and telephoned him a day or two later. By that time Joe had, of course, forgotten their names.

"Wanda?" he would repeat. "Oh yes, you're the blonde girl, aren't you?"

"No," she might say, "I'm the short fat girl with dark hair."

"Then fuck you!" he would reply and hang up.

Of course, wherever he took me Joe would embarrass me by saying "This is my friend, Henry Miller, *the writer*. You know—*Tropic of Cancer, The World of Sex. . . .*"

The person he was addressing often did not know the names Henry Miller, *Tropic of Cancer* and whatever, but would pretend with great gusto that they did. Some would even remind me that they had met me in Paris, London, Berlin or some out-of-the-way place in South America, all places which they themselves had never been to.

The question I was always asking at these parties was, "When do we eat?" Or, "Are we going to eat?" Joe would rustle up some food for me, one way or another. "You're always asking about food," he would say. "Listen, I brought you here to see the dames. Look at that one over there with the big teats! Do you want me to introduce you to her?"

"Do you know her?"

"Of course not. That doesn't make any difference here. Besides, you're a famous writer. They'll only be too happy to meet *you*. They'll piss in their pants. I *know* these bitches!"

What interested me in Joe Gray, more than all the cunts he brought to see me, was the joy and the appreciation he showed for the books he liked. Over his fireplace were lined up some of the most bewitching titles anyone might desire. When Joe read a book he devoured it hook, line and sinker, as we say. It stayed with him for days, weeks, months. Not only did he make notes and copy passages from his favorite works, but he read the books which the author may have mentioned in passing. (I know no better way to detect what books are worth reading.) Incidentally, let it be said in his favor there was only one other person I knew who collected and read wonderful books and that was John Cowper Powys. When I visited him in Wales my eye fell on the range of books beside me. I could read the titles clearly. They were all classics—Homer, Virgil, Dante, Villon, Rabelais, Dostoievsky, Shakespeare, Marlowe, Webster, the Greek dramatists, Ovid, Lucretius, Longinus, etc. I was rather surprised, I remember, and asked him (rather audaciously) if he ever looked at them now and then. To my amazement he replied: "Why Henry, I read them all once a year." And he read them all in their own language! Of course Powys was an exceptional individual. Reading and rereading the classics did not dry him up. On the contrary—they increased his lust for life.

What endeared me to Joe the reader was the reverent way he referred to certain writers. I shall never forget how he took to Richard Jefferies, author of *The Story of My Heart*. He carried that book with him wherever he went and was continually lending it to people, whether they wanted it or not.

I also remember his reaction on first reading Dostoievsky. "How come nobody ever told me about this guy before!" he exclaimed. "He's not a writer, he's a magician, a giant."

But the strangest thing was to see him working on a broad

with one of his favorite authors. For, as the reader must have surmised already, in Joe's eyes most cunts were "dumb cunts." To observe him making it with one of the latter say with a Dostoievsky in his mitt, was like watching the artful Dodger. If one of these cunts truly liked the book Joe had shoved on her he was ready to kiss her ass. It just wasn't in the cards for "dumb cunts" to appreciate the likes of Dostoievsky or Herman Hesse, another favorite of his.

In the way he took to authors and painters, so he took to women. It was incredible to hear him extol the virtues of some slob he had become fond of. "You don't know her," he would begin. "She may be a slob but you can *trust* her."

"How do you mean, Joe, *trust her?*"

"I mean if you're short and need help, go to her. She'll help any damn fool out—because she doesn't know any better. I've seen her shell out a hundred bucks to some worthless bastard who didn't deserve to wipe her ass.

"Sure, what if she *is* a hooker, she's a friend in need. She'll even give you a free fuck if she likes you."

Another one he might like because she was a health food addict like himself. And another because she loved dogs. "Between you and me," he would say, "I think she lets them fuck her. Byron is always sniffing her, if you ever noticed. Yeah, she sure loves dogs, but she hates cats and birds, can you beat it?"

Living in that crazy world called Hollywood he came to know lots of freaks, I mean real freaks who belonged in the side show. There was a female midget he took quite a fancy to. She interested him profoundly, largely, I believe, because she was a great reader.

The people he didn't like, and they were often Jews, strange to say, even his dog Byron didn't like either. As I said earlier,

Byron was partly human. He picked up things which even Joe's dumb broads never got wise to. He was a horny beast too. Always humping something—a leg, a piece of furniture, a palm tree or whatever. Yet Byron never had a good fuck in his life. Strange, considering that his lord and master was such an expert about cunt. The trouble was, as I gradually discovered, Joe didn't think the bitches available were good enough for Byron. Many of Joe's friends were on the look-out for the right bitch for Byron, but none ever came up with the right one. Byron was worth his weight in gold, as Joe would say.

When Joe took a job out of town he would leave the receiver off the hook so he could talk to Byron at odd hours. If he heard Byron bark at the sound of his voice Joe would carry on a one-sided conversation which even a dog fancier would find incredible. Often Joe lacked the price of a good meal, but not Byron. Byron ate only the best, the most expensive food. And that made Joe happy.

One day I happened to meet Joe coming out of his pad. He's all smiles, I notice.

"What happened, Joe," I say, "what makes you so happy?"

"Come along with me," he says. "I'm just walking up the street in hopes of running into a dame who lives on this block. I've been flirting with her . . ."

When I heard the word "flirting" I couldn't believe my ears.

"Yeah," he continues, "I think she's the romantic type. Good looker, dresses well, polite and all that."

"Tell me more," I said, wondering if this was going to be one of his infatuations.

"I can't tell you much," says Joe, "because I think it's finished already. I'm not her type."

He goes on to tell me how he happened to notice that she came home exactly the same time every evening. He would be walking his dog and thus run into her, as she lived only a few doors away.

One evening, instead of saying "Hi" and passing on, he stops and says "Hello beautiful, aren't you a little early this evening?"

She answered coldly, "Is it any of your business? Why do I see you outside my door every evening?"

"Because," says Joe, "I have a yen for you."

"Oh yeah," says she, "well stick it up your ass."

Somewhat surprised by this sort of language coming from her, Joe says, "Is that a nice way to talk to a gentleman?"

"Whoever told you you were a gentleman?" she retorts.

"Come now, *lady*," says Joe, "be human, I'm a neighbor of yours, don't you know that?"

"No I don't," she snaps. "Go and get lost."

At this moment Byron rushes up from somewhere and begins to paw Joe. Somehow Byron appeals to the girl. She softens a bit.

"Beautiful dog," she says. "Where did you get him?"

Here Joe makes up a long story just to keep her from running out on him.

The girl leans over to pat Byron. As she does so Joe pats her on the rump. The girl pretends not to notice. Joe quickly follows with a "Why don't you come to my place for a few minutes. I'll fix you a cup of tea or whatever."

To his surprise she falls in step with him and before you know it she's in his pad examining my watercolors on the wall.

"Are you a painter?" she asks.

"No," says Joe, "I'm in the films. I'm a stunt-man. Sometimes I stand in for Dean Martin."

That's all he needed to say. From then on the conversation quickly switched to more interesting things. Apparently, like all the rest, no sooner did she hear "films" than she melted. Joe

didn't have to make her any tea—she gulped down a few bour-
bons straight, flung her arms around him and groped for his
prick.

"It was like falling off a log," says Joe.

"What happened then—did you give her a quick lay?"

"No," he replied, "I decided to make her beg for it. I told her
to come back tomorrow. You'll see, tomorrow she'll be ringing
my doorbell, I know these cunts. She doesn't want me, she
wants a job in the movies. When she heard "Dean Martin" I
could see the change come over her. Maybe she thinks he'll give
her a quick lay and make a star of her. What shit! They never
learn."

"Where are we going, Joe?"

"Nowhere. I just wanted to give Byron a run."

In trying to give a full portrait of my friend I am afraid I have
magnified his faults and foibles.

Joe was one of the three best friends I ever had in America.
There was nothing he would not do for me if I needed his aid. He
was usually cheerful, if a bit feisty also. He liked and disliked
intensely. There was no in-between for him.

There were many people who referred to him as their friend,
but Joe was the sort who acknowledged only two or three
friends—the others were simply acquaintances, bar flies, and so
on.

If he disagreed with your opinion, he disagreed violently. He
was intense in everything. Above all, he hated hypocrites,
people who said one thing and meant another.

He did not hate women, he merely distrusted them. As for the
women themselves, they were attracted to him as if to some
magnet. Joe attributed a lot of this to the nose the plastic surgeon
had given him. But I am sure everything would have been just

the same had he never lost his old schnozzle. For Joe emanated warmth, enthusiasm, confidence. He never let anybody down. If he thought of himself as somewhat of a healer there was truth in the assumption. Everyone he came in contact with felt something unusual in Joe's vibrations. Even the men he worked for in the film studios acknowledged this gift.

He laughed easily and heartily. He never appeared if in a bad mood, nor did he have many bad moods.

I used to tell him he was a natural born healer, that he should have been a rabbi instead of a stunt man. Joe's method of healing was somewhat unusual: he healed through books. He kept a huge notebook of quotations from the books he read and when the opportunity presented itself he would read a few passages to the poor devil who was suffering. If one had told him that that was the method employed by Christian Scientists he would have scoffed.

All in all he was an original. No one ever forgot Joe Gray once they had a taste of him. Joe and his dog Byron. People would ask after Byron as if he were a human being. And Joe treated Byron like a human being.

It's been my good fortune always to have two or three good friends I could count on in time of need. To be blessed with just *one* good friend is usually sufficient. Friends more than made up (for me) the absence of money. And when I say friends I mean ordinary individuals, not exceptional ones. But they were exceptional in their ability to give, to serve, to be at one's beck and call. Nearly always these friends possessed a good sense of humor. They were never preachers or advisers. In fact there was always something a bit dotty or eccentric about them. One might say clownlike, I suppose. Above all, they were always unselfish. In Joe Gray's case he was unselfish where women were concerned.

That was not because he despised them but rather because he looked upon them as gifts from above. He may have treated them outwardly like dogs, but anyone who knew him knew differently. It wasn't cunt that put Joe at their mercy but the fact that he saw their angelic side. He was always trying to preserve them from some threat of harm or humiliation. In his own peculiar way he was a Knight of the Round Table. He was one *in disguise*. As for the friends Joe made, they were all *close* friends. He couldn't tolerate anything lukewarm. Because he had once been a professional boxer he sometimes took insults that were unbelievable. At the height of an altercation at a bar, for example, he would often grab me by the arm and say "Let's get out of here!" Outside I would say "What's the matter, Joe, why didn't you give him a poke in the jaw?" and Joe would always reply, "Because I'm not allowed to. Besides, he was too much of a punk for me to bother with. He had a big mouth, that's all."

Later, when I saw the film "A Bad Day at Black Rock," in which Spencer Tracy plays a one-armed man versed in jiu jitsu, I appreciated Joe's words. I also took another look at myself, I who usually relied on his ability to *talk his way* out of a bad situation.

People often asked me what Joe thought of films and film people. "It's a lot of shit," was his usual response. Nevertheless he had his heroes and heroines. John Garfield was one of them. Incidentally, Joe could have doubled for John Garfield. There was a more-than-usual resemblance between the two. Both lovable, especially with women, both handy with their fists, both genuine, both detesting sham and hypocrisy, both of humble origin and ghetto background. I mention John Garfield because, when pushed to the wall to name someone he admired in the films, John Garfield always came to his lips. The films he played in were like fragments of Joe's life.

Then there was George Raft. He and Joe had been friends for years. Joe always spoke highly of George Raft—a man one could rely on. Of course Raft had a strong appeal for women, as did Joe. And Raft was generous, a quality Joe never failed to admire.

One of the unusually bright days with Joe was spent in Big Sur. Bob Snyder was then making the documentary film of my life and all we needed was a glimpse of Big Sur. We brought with us Michiyo Watanabe, who had been living in my home in Pacific Palisades. I had not been back to Big Sur for ten years or more. It looked more attractive than ever, the little house on Partington Ridge. Of course my companions fell in love with the place. Who wouldn't? It was the nearest thing to Greece imaginable. We spent the night there and on the way home fell to singing old songs, like "Meet Me Tonight in Dreamland," "You Great Big Beautiful Doll," "Roses in Picardy," and such like. Even Michiyo, who had been born and raised in Japan, caught the spirit. It was a wonderful way to finish off an exciting trip. It also made Big Sur seem more precious than ever. (It was probably my very last trip there. My days of travel are over, along with my days of travail.)

As I have said before, Joe was not only a stunt man but a stand-in for Dean Martin. In photos they bore a remarkable resemblance to one another. Joe enjoyed working for Dean. On several occasions Joe had traveled abroad with him as well as to Mexico. Now Dean was getting ready to make a film in Mexico. It was a rough region but Joe liked the Mexicans and, besides, he was short of cash. So, in spite of his premonitions, he accompanied Dean to Mexico. In a few days, to my great surprise, he was back in L.A. To my even greater surprise he complained of not feeling right—was going to see a doctor. I say "surprise" because Joe was not only a healthy specimen but a health food addict, a believer in Dr. Bieler and absorbed as much sun and oxygen as he could.

Well, I believe that Dean urged him to see his own doctor—or perhaps it was Elizabeth Taylor's. I saw him the day after he entered the hospital—in the evening. He seemed (to me) fit as a fiddle. When I inquired what he was suffering from he couldn't tell me exactly—probably from the poor Mexican diet, he thought.

Anyway, the next day he was dead. He was in his late forties, a remarkable specimen of good health and *joie de vivre*. I never did learn what the doctors thought killed him.

His last words, it seemed, were about his dog Byron. I found out later that one of Dean Martin's daughters adopted Byron. Bless her! To this day people ask me, "What ever became of Byron?"

Henry astride his best friend, Pacific Palisades.

Chapter Eight

MY BEST FRIEND

Believe it or not, it was my bike. This one I had bought at Madison Square Garden, at the end of a six-day race. It had been made in Chemnitz, Bohemia and the six-day rider who owned it was a German, I believe. What distinguished it from other racing bikes was that the upper bar slanted down towards the handle bars.

I had two other bikes of American manufacture. These I would lend my friends when in need. But the one from the Garden no one but myself rode. It was like a pet. And why not? Did it not see me through all my times of trouble and despair?

Yes, I was in the throes of love, a first love, than which nothing is more disastrous, as a rule. My friends had become disgusted with me; they were deserting me, or *vice versa*, one by one. I was desolate and alone. Whether my parents knew of my sad plight I don't recall, but I am sure they knew that *something* was bothering me. That "something" was a beautiful young woman named Una Gifford, whom I had met during my high school days.

As I have told elsewhere, we were such naive creatures that perhaps we kissed two or three times—at a party, for example, never elsewhere. Though we both had telephones, we never telephoned one another. Why? I ask myself. (Because it would have been too bold perhaps.) We did write each other, but our letters were far apart. I remember how each day when I came home I turned first to the mantel piece, where letters were kept, and it was almost always a blank absence that greeted me.

It was a period when I spent most of my days job-hunting (presumably). Actually, I went to a movie or the burlesk, (if I could afford it). Suddenly I stopped doing this, *and* did nothing. Nothing but ride the bike. Often I was in the saddle, so to speak, from morning till evening. I rode everywhere and usually at a good clip. Some days, I encountered some of the six-day riders at the fountain in Prospect Park. They would permit me to set the pace for them along the smooth path that led from the Park to Coney Island.

I would visit old haunts, such as Bensonhurst, Ulmer Park, Sheepshead Bay and Coney Island. And always, no matter how diverse the scenery, I am thinking of *her*. Why doesn't she write me? When will the next party be? Etc., etc. I never had obscene thoughts about her, never dreamt of fucking her some day or even feeling her twat. No, she was like the princess in the fairy tale—untouchable even in dream.

Nor did it ever occur to me to ride to Greenspoint, where she lived, and ride up and down her street in the hope of catching a glance of her. Instead I rode to the faraway places, scenes associated with my childhood—and happy days.

I thought of those idyllic days ruefully, with a heavy heart. Where were they now, these dear pals of my early youth? Were they going through the same anguish as I—or were some of them married already perhaps?

Sometimes, after having finished a good book, I would think of nothing but the characters in that book. The characters I speculated about most were usually out of Dostoievsky's novels, particularly *The Idiot, The Brothers Karamazov* and *The Possessed.* Indeed they were no longer characters from a book, but living creatures, people who haunted my reveries and dream life. Thus, thinking of some absurd individual like Smerdyakov I would suddenly burst out laughing, only to quickly check myself and veer my thoughts toward her. It was impossible to rid my mind of her. I was obsessed, fascinated, bereaved. If by some great chance I may have run into her I would doubtless have been tongue-tied.

Oh yes, once in a blue moon I would receive a letter from her, usually from some summer resort where she was spending her vacation. It would always be a short letter, couched in conventional language—and, to my mind, completely devoid of feeling. And my reply would pretty much match her letter despite the fact that my heart was breaking.

Heart break! There was a subject I gave myself to totally. Did other people my age suffer the same pangs? Was first love always as painful, awkward and barren as this? Was I perhaps a special case, a "romantic" of the first water? The answers to these self-addressed queries were generally written in my friend's faces. The moment I mentioned her name a look of total uninterest would emanate from them. "Still thinking about her?" "Haven't you had enough already?" And so on. Implicit in their reactions was—how stupid can a guy become? And over a girl, no less.

As we spun along (me and my double) I went over these fundamental facts backwards and forwards. It was like studying a theorem in algebra. And never once did I run into a compassionate soul! I became so desolate that I took to calling my bike my friend. I carried on silent conversations with it. And of course I paid it the best attention. Which meant that everytime I returned home I stood the bike upside down, searched for a clean rag and polished the hubs and the spokes. Then I cleaned the chain and, greased it afresh. That operation left ugly stains on the stone in the walkway. My Mother would complain, beg me to put a newspaper under my wheel before starting to clean it. Sometimes she would get so incensed that she would say to me, in full sarcasm, "I'm surprised you don't take that thing to bed with you!" And I would retort—"I would if I had a decent room and a big enough bed."

That was another grievance I had to put up with—no room of my own. I slept in a narrow hall bedroom, decorated only by a shade to keep out the early morning light. If I read a book it was at the dining room table. I never used the parlor except to listen to phonograph records. It was when listening to some of my favorite records (in the gloomy parlor) that I would go through the greatest anguish about her. Each record I put on the machine only deepened my sorrow. The individual who moved me the most—from ecstasy to absolute despair—was the Jewish Cantor Sirota. Next to him came Amato, the baritone at the Metropolitan Opera. And after these came Caruso and John McCormack, the beloved Irish tenor.

I took care of my wheel as one would look after a Rolls Royce. If it needed repairs I always brought it to the same shop on Myrtle Avenue run by a Negro named Ed Perry. He handled the bike with kid gloves, you might say. He would always see to it that neither front nor back wheel wobbled. Often he would do a job for me without pay, because, as he put it, he never saw a man so in love with his bike as I was.

There were streets I avoided and streets I favored. In some streets the setting or the architecture actually gave me a lift.

There were sedate streets and run-down ones, streets full of charm and others horrendously dull. (Didn't Whitman say somewhere, "Architecture is what you do to it when you look at it"?) As a dromomaniac I was able to carry on an elaborate interior dialogue and at the same time be aware of the stage setting through which I was moving. Riding the bike was a little different; I had to watch my p's and q's or take a bad spill.

About this time the champion sprinter was Frank Kramer, whom of course I idolized. Once I managed to stay right behind him during one of his practice spins from Prospect Park to Coney Island. I remember him slapping me on the back when I caught up with him and, as he slapped my back, said, "Good work, young feller—keep it up!" That day was a red letter day in my life. For once I forgot about Una Gifford and gave myself up to dreams of riding in Madison Square Garden some day, along with Walter Rutt, Eddie Root, Oscar Egg and the other celebrities of the track.

After a time, habituated to spending so many hours a day on my bike, I became less and less interested in my friends. My wheel had now become my one and only friend. I could rely on it, which is more than I could say about my buddies. It's too bad no one ever photographed me with my "friend." I would give anything now to know what we looked like.

Years later in Paris, I got myself another bike, but this one was an everyday sort, with brakes. To slow up demanded an effort on the part of one's legs. I could have had hand brakes put on my handle bars but that would have made me feel like a sissy. It was dangerous and thrilling to race through the city streets at top speed. Fortunately the automobile was not then much in evidence. What one really had to watch out for were youngsters playing in the middle of the street.

Mothers would warn their children to be careful, to keep their eyes open for that crazy young man who loves to speed through the streets. In other words I soon became a terror in the neighborhood.

I was both a terror and a delight. The kids were all begging their parents to get them a bike like mine.

How long can the heart ache without bursting? I have no idea. I only know that I put in a grueling period courting a girl *in absentia*. Even on my 21st birthday—a great event in my life—I sat some distance apart from her, too timid to open my mouth and tell her of my love. The last time I saw her was shortly after, when I plucked up the courage to ring her doorbell and tell her I was leaving for Juneau, Alaska, to become a placer miner.

It was almost harder to separate from my wheel from Chemnitz, Bohemia. I must have given it to one of my cronies, but to whom, I no longer remember.

It should be borne in mind that, although my heart was breaking, I could still enjoy a good laugh. When I had the dough, I would often take in a vaudeville show at the Palace or spend the afternoon at the Houston Street Burlesk or some other burlesk house. The comedians from these shows were later to become figures in radio and television. In other words, I could literally laugh on the wrong side of my face. It was this ability to laugh in spite of everything that saved me. I had already known that famous line from Rabelais—"For all your ills I give you laughter." I can say from personal experience that it is a piece of the highest wisdom. There is so precious little of it today—it's no wonder the drug pushers and the psychoanalysts are in the saddle.

Finis.